FANTASY ENCOUNTER GAMES

BOOKS BY HERBERT A. OTTO

Guide to Developing Your Potential
Group Methods Designed To Actualize
 Human Potential: A Handbook
More Joy in Your Marriage
Explorations in Human Potentialities (Editor)
Ways of Growth (Editor, with John Mann)
Human Potentialities: The Challenge and the Promise (Editor)
The Family: In Search of a Future (Editor)
The New Sexuality (Editor)
Love Today: A New Exploration (Editor)
Total Sex (with Roberta Otto)

Herbert A. Otto

FANTASY ENCOUNTER GAMES

Harper & Row, Publishers
New York, Evanston, San Francisco, London

*This volume is dedicated to the
Human Potentialities Movement, the
humanistic psychologists, and all
those who know that the actualizing
of their potential is a lifelong
exciting adventure.*

This book was originally published in hardcover by
Nash Publishing Corp. It is here reprinted by arrangement.

FANTASY ENCOUNTER GAMES

First HARPER & ROW edition published 1974.

STANDARD BOOK NUMBER: 06–465003–0

CONTENTS

PREFACE

The work in the area of fantasy development began in 1963 during the beginning years of my work with Developing Personal Potential groups at the University of Utah. From these early explorations, conducted as a part of the Human Potentialities Research Project at Utah, grew the concept of fantasy gaming as a means of developing the imagination.

I want to thank my classes at the University of Utah as well as members of marathon weekends I have conducted in different parts of the country, who directly and indirectly contributed ideas. Members of the two Fantasy Weekends conducted at Esalen Institute in 1968 and 1969 were especially helpful in the course of two very challenging and mind expanding experiences. Gwen Davis of Chicago, the editorial assistant on the initial written development of these games offered valuable skilled assistance. Finally, I wish to thank my wife, Roberta, for her warm help and support throughout this project.

HERBERT A. OTTO.
Chicago, Ill./La Jolla, Calif.

FANTASY ENCOUNTER GAMES

INTRODUCTION

Imagination is more important than knowledge.
—Albert Einstein

Fantasy Encounter Games are for enjoyment.

Life is a journey into fantasy and imagination. By nourishing and developing our capacity to fantasize, we enrich and expand life itself. Our horizons are limited only by our imagination.

Adult play is important. We need to play more to recreate ourselves, to regenerate, to allow ourselves more pleasure and to recharge our energies so that we can actualize more of our potential.

The Fantasy Encounter Games are a new and revolutionary way of interpersonal gaming. They are designed not only to enlarge the horizon of our fantasies by letting our imaginations play, but offer a new adventure in communication.

Many of the games combine the enjoyment of play with the opportunity to broaden self-awareness and gain new insights and self-understanding.

Before the advent of television, many parents read stories aloud to their children. There was considerable listening to radio programs with plot lines of adventure and action. These practices fostered the exercise of imagination and fantasy. *Television with its detailed visual presentation provides raw material for the imagination, but at the same time muffles the active exercise of fantasy.* We are content to watch someone else's fantasy on the screen. For this reason, it is more important today than ever that adults and children enjoy the process of fantasy. Limiting or neglecting the flow of fantasy and imagination cuts to the very roots of man's vitality and creativity.

Sharing fantasies is a freeing and joyous activity. Today only a handful of people have experienced the freedom and joy of communicating their fantasies. Most of these people have been through certain forms of sensitivity training or encounter groups, or have attended experiences at growth centers such as Esalen Institute, California, Oasis in Chicago or Aureon in New York City. They have discovered that verbal sharing of fantasies adds a new freedom, new depth and spontaneity to their communication. (A list of growth centers which offer experiences designed to actualize human potential and foster personality growth has been placed in Appendix A, at the back of this book.)

Everyone daydreams and fantasizes, but these activities are often denied or repressed. They are a normal and natural part of the ongoing process we call personality and are needed to maintain man's vital functioning.

For years we have been told to "stop daydreaming and pay attention!" As a result of these repeated warnings a guilt structure has been induced, and many people feel guilty as soon as they become aware of their daydreams or fantasizing. Science has recently discovered that dreaming is an important activity of the human psyche. Subjects in a laboratory who are awakened every time they begin to dream (the moment they begin to dream can be determined by eyeball movements) suffer from unpleasant personality disturbances and symptoms of dysfunction. Some scientists believe that dreams represent a form of "data processing." It is clear that dreams serve a function; in a similar manner so do daydreaming and fantasizing.

A distinction must be made, however, between daydreaming and fantasizing. Daydreams are undirected fleeting images, reveries and idea fragments which flow as an ongoing undifferentiated stream of ideational activity. A major characteristic of daydreams is that they are very quickly forgotten and generally seem too fleeting to merit communicating to another person. *On the other hand I define fantasy as a conscious form of shaping, forming, expressing and enjoying the free flow of imagination.* By fantasizing, I mean the creative process involved in the consciously directed, shaped flow of images and ideational material, usually united by a common theme. In short, fantasizing is the *directed* flight of imagination. Fantasies appear to have a more pronounced emotional thrust than daydreams. Fantasies which have a strong emotional investment, when communicated, can serve as a springboard for recognizing and working out feelings, and for gaining new awareness.

Although everyone fantasizes, very few people have the courage to put their fantasies into words and communicate them. It appears that the guilt feelings attendant on sexual fantasizing irradiate the whole field of fantasy activity and act as an inhibitor. Recognition of this can enhance fantasy productivity. There is no question that an important aspect of freedom and intimacy in communication involves the sharing of fantasies and ultimately sexual fantasies. By using fantasy encounter games, *the ability to share fantasies is developed. This adds a new dimension and depth to communication.*

Fantasy can have another function: It can be a form of direct communication with the unconscious. Often, a fantasy about a person, which is shared with that person, appears to communicate directly to the unconscious. In my weekend marathons entitled "Developing Personal Potential" we use fantasies extensively. Usually no effort is made by the recipient to analyze the fantasy given to him by another person. Yet there have been innumerable instances of insight, crystallizing and working out of feelings due to a fantasy which was recognized as important weeks or months after a weekend group experience.

The deliberate cultivation of our ability to fantasize is highly desirable for a number of additional reasons. Not only does the process of fantasizing stimulate, expand and nourish the development of our imagination, but *fantasy replenishes and nourishes man's hope.* All of us live with the hope that at least some of our fantasies will be realized, and in this sense, imagination and reality are not necessarily separate worlds. One of the true functions of fantasy is as a stepping stone to reality. Through the process of *verbalizing,* we externalize a fantasy. In turn, through this process, elements of the externalized fantasy are more strongly incorporated into the "wish" or "desire" structure of the individual, and can become motivational forces; they can even become recognized as desirable goals. Thus, the verbalization of a fantasy can have a definite, measurable impact on reality. Fantasies motivate us in our course through life—although some persons will have difficulty admitting this.

Use of the fantasy also becomes a way of reaching and expanding deeper levels of the self. Through a study of our fantasy stream we can attain new awareness and self-understanding. We can discover unknown aspects of the self (the fantasy self) and by integrating these aspects with those which are known, bring about a greater wholeness and synthesis of the self. In this sense, fantasizing is both a form of giving to oneself and giving to others.

By sharing our fantasy with others, we embark on the adventure of self-disclosure which can lead to greater authenticity and the development of trust in our interpersonal relationships. We learn that people not only accept our fantasies, but in many instances, consider them a gift which enables them to grow in turn.

Be free! Have joy! Fantasize!

HOW TO PLAY THE GAMES

There is a wide variety among the games. Whatever your mood and sense of adventure, there is a game to add new dimensions to your experience. When you are ready for the excitement of fantasy encounter games, select the one(s) you would most like to play.

Four major categories are offered:

Fantasy Games for Two

These are "duo-games" to be played on a date, or with a friend, acquaintance or family. Two and sometimes three people can participate. Some of these games are for indoor use; others can be played outdoors—while out walking for example. Some of these games can also be played in a group. They are marked ALSO A GROUP GAME in the upper right-hand corner.

Sensory Fantasy Games

These are exciting games for two or more people which focus on the use of specific senses, or multiple sensory experiencing, as a means of expanding fantasy and imagination.

Group Fantasy Games

These are a series of enjoyable games designed to introduce a group of four or more persons to the new dimension of fantasy encounters. Most of the games are for home use.

Fantasy and Imagination—On Your Own

There are games to be played alone. Some of the games offer an opportunity to expand self-awareness and understanding in the context of developing the imagination and fostering creativity.

Ground Rules

The more you play fantasy encounter games, the more you will enjoy them. Every game contains complete instructions, and there are certain basic ground rules which can greatly add to your enjoyment:

A. Most of the games are designed to be played with a partner. To be fair, toss a coin to decide which of you has the first turn for fantasy play.

B. Games are divided into Part I, Part II and so on. Some of the games lend themselves to letting partners take turns on completion of each part. This can make the game livelier and faster moving.

C. Some games have a section entitled *Partner Action*. This is designed to allow the partner to participate in the fantasy by injecting new adventure and new inputs into the game. To preserve the element of surprise, you are urged *not* to read these sections. You will have more fun playing the games this way. The words "PARTNER ACTION" appear next to the titles of these games.

D. It seems to be helpful for many people to close their eyes while they are creating their fantasies. Encourage your partner to close his or her eyes.

E. To add additional excitement and spontaneity and to introduce team creativity, "The Fantasy Acceleration Technique" has been placed in Appendix B. *Only* after you have played several fantasy games should you read this technique for even more delightful gaming.

LET YOUR ENCOUNTER WITH FANTASY BE A SOURCE OF PLEASURE AND JOY!

FANTASY GAMES FOR TWO

Duo-fantasy games are games designed for any two or three people who want to enjoy themselves while expanding their imagination. Two friends or any couple spending time together can choose from among all the games, each fitting a different mood and occasion. Each game is unique! Some games can be played at home; others are "Walking Games" to be played while walking about town (or for a night on the town).

When you and your partner want to play duo-fantasy games, read them over together. Each of you choose the one game that appeals to you most, then go ahead and play.

It is usually best to play no more than two or three games at a time. Fantasy games should never be forced—both partners must want to play.

Enjoy!

THE COSMIC VISITORS ARRIVAL FANTASY

This is an exciting, action-type fantasy. It is a *walking fantasy* and can be played while walking through the streets. Players of this fantasy game are offered an opportunity to look at the world and human beings through the eyes of intelligent visitors from outer space. As a result of this experience, players see the world and people emerge in a different perspective; certain things taken for granted may now appear in a new light.

Background

Both partners in this game are assumed to be cosmic visitors from the same planet or source in space, who are now visiting Earth. Each of you has arrived on Earth in a different vehicle and landed in a different area. On the way to Earth you probably have had some interesting adventures.

Both of you have assumed human form. *You are inhabiting the bodies of the two persons who are reading about this fantasy.* The personality of the person whose body you are inhabiting is not injured or impeded in any way and continues to function, except that now you, the cosmic visitor, are in command. As the cosmic visitor, you will employ the body of your host to learn more about Earth and its inhabitants.

Outline: Part I—Arrival

A. Begin by one of you sharing something about your tribe and organization, the location of your landing field on the planet Earth from which you have come to this city.

Share some reminiscences about your home planet or base.

Now give the other cosmic visitor a chance to tell yo about himself:

B. Discuss your voyage to Earth:

What adventures did you have?

How did Earth look to you as you approached it?

Outline: Part II

C. Tell how you landed:

Was your craft injured?

Tell how you made your way to this city by taking over various human and animal forms. (Be specific as to why you took over the body of the person you are currently inhabiting.)

How did you take over this body?

What was he doing when you took over?

Outline: Part III—Arrival Activity

Both of you can now observe the human beings and their customs. Walk to specific places to observe them such as restaurants, stores, bus stops, and the like. Feel free to ask each other questions about what you observe. For example:

Why do people hurry so?

Why do they rarely look at each other except with a passing glance?

Why do human beings dress the way they do?

Is there some sense behind the various activities of people?

Sample some of the strange foods, drink some beverages of the Earth people. Try to understand why they behave in certain ways and what they think about.

THE COSMIC VISITORS MISSION FANTASY

This is another action fantasy game to deepen your understanding of the Earth people. It can be played while walking through the streets of a town, or at home. Copies of the questions (see Part II) should be in the possession of each player for the game.

Background

You are both cosmic visitors from outer space with the same background as in the Cosmic Visitors Arrival Fantasy. Please read the Arrival Fantasy together for full understanding of your mission (see page 12).

Outline: Part I

In order to get better acquainted, you may wish to tell each other about some of your adventures while you visited other planets on the way to Earth.

How is the Earth planet different from the last planet you visited?

Outline: Part II

You have already established that you are on separate missions to Earth, but you cannot divulge to each other what your mission is. However, each of you have been given an identical set of questions which you seek to answer on your visit to Earth. These questions form guidelines for your visit to this planet, and the answers you obtain are relevant to your mission.

Questions About Human Beings

1. What do human beings like best? Why?

2. What do they like least? Why?

3. What do they consider their best social structure (government)? Does it work? Why? If not, why not?

4. Who are the true leaders of the human beings? Why?

5. What is the potential of the human being?

6. What is on the minds of human beings? Is it different from what they talk about when they meet each other?

7. In your opinion, will the human beings destroy themselves with the weaponry which they have developed? Why?

8. How do human beings feel about other human beings who differ from them in some ways, for example, those who talk in different ways or have different skin pigmentation? Why do they feel this way about them?

9. Are the human beings likely to contaminate space or the universe?

10. What do most human beings believe happens when they become nonfunctional (die)? Why?

11. Which of Earth's other inhabitants do human beings like best? Which animals or insects?

12. Do human beings love the planet they live on?

13. What is the greatest threat to the survival of the human beings?

Outline: Part III

In your capacity as cosmic visitors, ask some of the above questions *of friends and acquaintances of the people whose bodies you temporarily inhabit.* If you want to, take notes about these answers. You may also want to walk about to observe people and base your answers on these observations. Each partner could take turns sharing his reactions to questions he selects (or take each question in turn).

Outline: Part IV

Finally, you may wish to override your instructions (why?) and share what your true mission on Earth is (was) with your partner. Was it your mission

A. To destroy Earth if you thought it would endanger other civilizations or life forms in the Universe?

B. To observe Earth as a scientist and report?

C. To help the Earth people?

FANTASY GIFTS

This is a very simple lively fantasy game. It is a walking game which can be played as you are wandering along a downtown street window-shopping. It can be a quick fun game if you desire, or a means to greater awareness and understanding.

Background

As you walk along, ask yourself, "What gift would I choose for my partner and present to him (her) right now if I had all the money I needed to do so?" Choose a gift from the window displays that you see. Present it to your partner by showing him the gift and telling him why you chose it.

Outline: Part I

To begin this game, give your partner any gift you want to (by pointing it out) in the display window of the next shop you come to. Do it spontaneously.

Outline: Part II

A Symbolic Gift: The Gift that is YOU

Select the gift that from your point of view, represents or symbolizes your partner. Give him this imaginational gift by pointing it out.

Tell your partner why this gift symbolizes him.

For example, Mary presented a brightly colored, plaid jacket to Jim. She remarked:

> "I see you as a very colorful, energetic person. You are sort of pleasantly rough like the tweed. You are complex like the plaid patterns. Sometimes you have a British accent and this is a Scotch plaid."

Jim gave Mary a ruby necklace as the "gift that is you." He simply said:

> "The color red means warmth and love to me. It's a beautiful necklace and so are you. It has great value, and I value you greatly. It is very intricate. All this is you."

Outline: Part III

A Symbolic Gift: The Gift that Describes our Relationship

Give your partner a gift that describes your relationship as you see it and tell him why you think it does.

Jim chose a round loaf of rye bread. He said:

"This bread symbolizes our relationship—where it is right now. I find that being together is nourishing and good for both of us. We grow by it. It has a wonderful texture like the crust on the bread. Our relationship is round as a circle and yet has imperfections just like the bread. But they don't matter—they are a part of the bread."

Mary picked an abstract painting and commented on its features:

"The whole thing is beautiful and colorful—we are that shape. The future is that bright area over there. The dark area is what we still have to learn about each other."

A Symbolic Gift: The Gift that Describes How I Feel Right Now

Pick a gift to give to your partner which is symbolic of your feelings at this moment—then tell what you are feeling.

For example, Mary chose a dress made of very bright, shimmering material. She said:

"Right now I am feeling fully alive, very bright, happy, lively, energetic, glad to be with you."

DO YOUR OWN THING FANTASY

Today "doing your own thing," (doing what you really want to do) is becoming increasingly important to a growing number of people. Almost everyone occasionally fantasizes about doing their own thing. This game offers an opportunity to explore this very important fantasy area—an area which not only nourishes hope but which can provide us with the springboard of motivation. A pleasurable and joyous experience is ahead for you.

Background

Imagine that only an hour ago you were informed that you held the winning ticket in the New York State lottery. Suddenly financial independence has arrived for you, no longer a dream but a fact. You are finally in a position *to do what you really want to do*—" to do your own thing."

Outline: Part I

Ask yourself this question:

"What is it that I really want to do now?"

If you feel you want to travel the world first, assume you are back from your travels and you are now confronted with the many possibilities of doing your own thing.

Begin with your work or daily activities. What changes would you bring about? (Remember you have the means at your disposal to establish yourself independently.)
What changes would there be

In your home? (furnishings?)
Location of home? (new place?)
Mode of transportation?
Mode of dress?
Other changes?

Outline: Part II

Develop your fantasy around the following questions:
How would doing your own thing affect your friends and acquaintances?

Would they be included in some way?
What would their reactions be?
What about parents and relatives?
Your immediate family?

DO NOT READ BEYOND THIS POINT. LET YOUR
PARTNER'S ACTION BRING YOU THE SURPRISE
OF NEW ADVENTURE.

Partner Action

Use your empathy and understanding to help your partner find out what doing his own thing means to him.

If necessary, clarify for your partner that for most people, eating, drinking, sleeping and amusing themselves is not enough. This does not mean that the option of "playboy" or "playgirl" is not open. But is this enough for your partner— *does it represent what he really wants to do?* If your partner chooses to be a playboy or -girl ask him about the things he would do. Encourage him to talk about this in considerable detail—perhaps plan a year of what he would do.

For the most part people appear to find their greatest satisfaction in some kind of creative activity which "turns them on" or in activity or productivity which is deeply personally satisfying or enjoyable.

ALSO A GROUP GAME

THE FESTIVAL AND CELEBRATION FANTASY

Almost everyone enjoys festivals and celebrations. Unfortunately there are all too few such events on our journey through life. Yet festivals and celebrations are creative happenings which we can shape and bring into being, simply because we enjoy them. "Excuses," reasons or occasions for festivals and celebrations can always be found *once we have decided to allow ourselves this pleasure*. Invariably, celebrations begin with an idea. This fantasy game offers the vicarious experience of creating a celebration. The fantasy is also great fun for group gaming.

Background

Regardless of the resources at one's command, festivals and celebrations are a possibility if the right frame of mind or attitude emerges or is created. This fantasy game can be an experience for fostering your creative ingenuity within the framework of your life-style and in the here-and-now. It can also involve the free and limitless play of your imagination in an as-if situation. Whichever direction you choose, this game will be a positive experience, an encounter with good feelings and the glow of pleasure.

Outline: Part I

Any excuse is a good one for celebrating. *You* are having a celebration, party or festival because:

A. You gave a stray pussycat some water.

B. You found a beautiful outfit at a bargain.

C. You wrote that letter you've been wanting to write.

D. You heard a bird sing this morning and it was beautiful.

E. Your birthday is two months away.

F. It's good to be alive and to have friends.

G. Make up your own reason.

Now decide for yourself which would be more fun: to create a fantasy for a festival, party or celebration involving where you are right now in your life (taking into account your current economic standing), the *here-and-now route,* OR, to create a festival or celebration as if you had un-limited, or certain specific funds at your disposal for this occasion, the *as-if route.*

Remember, if you are creating a fantasy for a celebration or party based on where you are in the here-and-now, do not let economic considerations ("It will cost too much") keep you from embarking on this type of fantasy. It is possible to have great parties for little money. Just let your ingenuity play—how about a "bring your own wine bottle" for a wine tasting party? OR a beer tasting party with everyone bringing two bottles or more of imported beer? ("Economic reasons" are too often used by people as "cop-outs" thereby denying themselves the pleasure of a celebration.)

Outline: Part II

Now that you have decided which route to choose in this fantasy game, build a fantasy of a celebration, festival or party which you would like to give. Provide as much detail as possible including

> Music and/or dancing
> Food and refreshments
> Games
> Creative happenings
> Decor or festive decorations

You may wish to make brief notes as your ideas emerge. NOTICE: THIS CAN BE A FANTASY GAME IN WHICH BOTH PARTNERS SHARE OR EACH MAY SHAPE HIS OWN SEPARATE FANTASY. IT IS ALSO GREAT FUN FOR GROUP GAMING.

For Group Use

If this game is to be used in a group, ask someone to volunteer to take notes of the major ideas as the group develops the fantasy. Someone also needs to take responsibility for stimulating the group to explore specifics. For example, if the group decides to go the here-and-now route and someone suggests having a rock band, ask:

> "Do we know of any rock band that would play for free—or for what possible cost?"

If the group goes the as-if route and suggests music, ask:

> "What band—the Stones? The Who? and so on.

(It may also be fun to draw up budgets for the here-and-now and as-if fantasies.)

FOR MAXIMUM EFFECTIVENESS IN THIS GAME,
DO NOT READ AHEAD UNTIL YOU HAVE
COMPLETED PART II.

Outline: Part III (Optional)

As a conclusion to this game discuss the following
question:

> "Should we move in the direction of having a
> celebration, festival or party in the near future
> (using the ideas we have dreamed up in this
> game)?"

THE REINCARNATION
FANTASY

This may be either a short fantasy experience or a more
lengthy one depending on your background and inclination.
Again, depending on your philosophy and attitude, the Reincarnation Fantasy can be a very engrossing guessing game
and exploration which may well furnish you with clues about
your own possible previous incarnations.

Background

Reincarnation—the belief that a person may be born and
reborn a number of times—is an important part of many
oriental religions, including Buddhism and Brahmanism.
According to some of these doctrines man is chained to the

"wheel of life" and may even be reborn as an animal depending on the nature of his deeds and his ability to overcome illusion and karma. Recent research by well-known scholars both in the East and West has been concerned with the study and documentation of the reincarnation hypothesis. Many interesting case histories in support of this theory have been uncovered. Some subscribers to the reincarnation theory believe that they have some knowledge and clues as to their previous incarnations.

Outline: Part I

Ask yourself the following questions to help you enter the reincarnation fantasy:

A. Approximately how many rebirths have you had? (Let a number enter your mind.) Share as many of these reincarnations with your partner as you wish.

B. What was your vocation during these reincarnations—were you a peasant, a famous historic figure, a soldier, an artist, someone holding high office? Anything else?

C. In your reincarnation were you at any time of a different sex than you are now? If so, who were you?

D. Were you ever reborn as an animal?

NOTICE: YOU MAY WISH TO TAKE TURNS AFTER EACH PART OF THE GAME IS COMPLETED.

Outline: Part II

After you have finished your adventure with Part I of the Reincarnation Fantasy, ask your partner his reactions to your

total fantasy stream. What are *his* feelings about these reincarnations? Do some seem more plausible?

Outline: Part III

To conclude this experience you may wish to follow your
imagination and fantasy in response to the following
question:

"What may be my next rebirth, or what is the
prospect for me on leaving this life?"

It is now your partner's turn.

THE CHILDHOOD TREASURE

Did you ever as a child have an object that meant a great
deal to you—that you particularly treasured?

Background

Most children have had specific objects which they have
treasured at certain ages while growing up. It is fun to recall
one of these treasures and to weave a fantasy around it.

Outline: Part I

Each of you can share the story of a "treasure" you had as
a child.

A. Was it some object you discovered or found?

Was it a present given to you?

Was it a favorite toy, a stone, a marble, a doll, a teddy bear, a ring, or. . . ?

If you cannot recall, imagine what it might have been.

B. Try to recall details: How did the object look?

What was its color and so on?

What were the details leading up to the acquiring of your "treasure"?

C. Share the feelings you had about this object.

Outline: Part II

Build a fantasy around what has happened to your favorite treasure.

Where is it now?

Outline: Part III

Fantasize to whom you would give this treasure today if you had it. Share this fantasy.

THE FANTASY NEWS GAME

To enjoy this fantasy game, all you need is access to a radio during the time you spend with your partner.

Background

The objective of the game is to build your own fantasy story around a news item which you have picked.

Outline: Part I

Listen to the news broadcast together (every half-hour or on the hour on most stations). As you listen, pick a news item that appeals to you. Take notes if you want. Do not tell your partner which news story you are picking until you begin the game.

Outline: Part II

Partners can decide to compete to see who can make his fantasy the

> most gruesome
> most delightful
> funniest
> saddest
> most improbable
> most commonplace.

One of the above categories can be selected for each successive newscast. For example, if you pick "the funniest" category, each partner will make the news item which he has picked into a funny fantasy story, and try to produce a funnier one than his partner.

Jim and Frances started out the fantasy news game by selecting the category "the most commonplace." They decided to see which one of them could get the largest number of commonplace expressions or clichés into their fantasy. Frances chose to elaborate on a news story of a woman who was seriously injured in a car accident. She told at length about the woman's hospitalization, using as many commonplace expressions as she could:

> "And how is our patient this morning," said the doctor. "Roll over," said the nurse, and the like.

Finally Frances ended her story with the commonplace:

> "And she got well and lived happily ever after."

Jim, in turn, pursued the career of a man wanted for murder, who in Jim's fantasy became a dishwasher hiding from the police. The man led a prosaic life among all the dirty dishes of a "greasy spoon cafe." He died of old age. (By mutual consent, Frances won this one.)

Outline: Part III (Optional)

Another way to play the fantasy news game is not to compete with each other but instead to have each partner pick a different category that best fits the news item he has selected. For example, one partner could strive to make his fantasy "the saddest"; the other partner could elect to make his "the most improbable."

THE LOVING FANTASY

In today's competitive culture where pressure, anxiety, dehumanization and estrangement are the order of the day, much of our emotional and ideational preoccupation with people reflects the tempo of our time. This game is a beautiful fantasy experience which can leave you with a warm loving glow!

Background

It is perhaps safe to say that most people spend a comparatively small segment of their time letting themselves have loving thoughts (and loving feelings) about people who are close to them other than members of their family. When we do think about other people, our thoughts appear to center mostly around the mechanics of daily interaction, "news items" about people, with some dwelling on their shortcomings, weakness and problem areas. This game offers an opportunity to use fantasy to have a very positive experience relating to people who matter to us.

Outline: Part I

Before starting the experience, it is best to read over all parts of this fantasy.

Think about the people you know and identify the people who matter to you.

Make a list (or mental list) of these people. (Many players prefer to close their eyes and take five minutes of silent time to do this).

Outline: Part II

Now select one person and have a loving fantasy about that person. Ask yourself this question: "Supposing I had the power of a magician or wizard, what is the most loving gift I could give this person?" (Read ahead to Part III before beginning the game.) For example, Fran made these comments:

> "As I think about Jack, the most loving thing I can do for him would be to give him $100,000. This would really make him happy and make him feel secure. He is a broker and this would be the right sum. If I gave him more, he would become prideful and self-important. In my opinion that's what he needs now to make his business and homelife really go."

> "I would give Ben a best seller and more love and caring from his wife."

> "To Carl I would give the ability to get out of his rut. He is stuck to his home and office routine too closely. I would give him the spirit of adventure and freedom so that he would travel more, attend conferences that interest him and take more risk by physical movement into this world. That's my loving fantasy for Carl."

Outline: Part III (Optional)

For a deeper experience before you explore the possibilities of a fantasy gift for a specific person, *close your eyes, think of his personality strengths and sources, his abilities and positive qualities.* If you wish, let yourself have loving feelings and thoughts about this person.

Only then proceed to explore the possibilities of the loving fantasy.

Now share your loving fantasy with your partner.

PARTNER ACTION

THE SUCCESS FANTASY

Success has been called a "bitch-goddess" by some and all too often can be likened to the carrot suspended in front of the donkey which keeps pursuing this ever-elusive goal. Some people view success as a by-product, the result of much creativity wedded to a considerable investment of effort and perseverance. Regardless of how we define success almost everyone has, at some time or another, entered into success fantasies. These are rarely verbalized. Yet verbally sharing a success fantasy can be a very positive, freeing experience. This game offers such an opportunity.

Background

Often people have success fantasies which may have nothing to do with their current occupation, interests or way of life. An example of this is the executive who has little or no interest in contemporary music but whose success fantasy is being a widely acclaimed rock singer.

For others, success fantasies are closely linked to vocation or life-style. In this latter instance, the success fantasy is often an extrapolation or something that *could* happen "if the breaks were right," if the person having the fantasy invested more time and energy, and so on.

Regardless of their nature, success fantasies usually serve a valuable function: They provide a positive input and they can nourish hope. Best of all, they can help us expect more from life than we are currently experiencing. In turn we may be motivated to initiate life-affirmative change.

Outline: Part I

Ask yourself the following questions:

How would I like to succeed at this point in my life?

What would be the greatest possible success for me?

Imagine that at this moment in your life fortune smiles, you "get the breaks," things really start coming your way. You can achieve the success you have always wanted. What would this success be?

Begin by going into as much detail as you can about the steps you see taking place (or which you make happen) which lead to this success.

Share what you see as the processes or sequences leading to your success.

Outline: Part II

Only after you have described in detail the sequence of events leading to your success, tell about the nature of your success. *(Keep your partner in suspense by leading up to your success gradually, step by step.)*

Outline: Part III

When you have told about your success go fully into these questions:

A. What is the reaction of the people who know you—family, relatives, friends, those with whom you work?

B. How would you change your present way of life now that you have achieved success?

C. How does success make you feel now that you have achieved it?

DO NOT READ BEYOND THIS POINT. LET YOUR PARTNER'S ACTION BRING YOU THE SURPRISE OF NEW ADVENTURE.

Partner Action: Part I

A. Encourage your partner to share his Success Fantasy, whatever it may be. Assure him that you will not laugh at it regardless of the nature of his fantasy. Point out that this is a fun game—anything goes. Tell him that if he wants you to, you will keep his Success Fantasy to yourself.

B. Ask him if he would like to close his eyes and take time to let his fantasy go into the sequences leading to his success.

Partner Action: Part II, Part III

A. Ask such questions as, "Would you give any special gifts to any friends or acquaintances now that you've made it and to celebrate your success?"

"What would you give me?"

B. As a conclusion, ask your partner this question: "How do you feel now that you have finished this fantasy encounter game?"

THE GYPSY FANTASY

"Everyone has a bit of the gypsy in him." This is an experience of discovering the gypsy in you. A fast-paced fantasy, it allows you to travel to any spot you choose in the world.

Background

> This is a fantasy for people who have the wander-lust or who would like to have it.

Imagine that a very distant relative has died and you have come into a major bequest, a sum of money which will enable you to travel wherever you want to go.

Outline: Part I

As an opener, are you interested in visiting spots of your childhood? (Close your eyes for better recall.)
OR
Places you have been to once before that you have always wanted to revisit?

Fantasize your trip to these places.

What would you find?

Outline: Part II

You are now ready to play the gypsy some more and wander further.

Where would you go?

How would you do it? (Would you drive or fly? What side-trips would you take?) Since you have the funds, what friends would you invite (in the event you would like company on this trip)?

DO NOT READ BEYOND THIS POINT. LET YOUR PARTNER'S ACTION BRING YOU THE SURPRISE OF NEW ADVENTURE.

Partner Action: Part I

Ask these questions:

A. What people would you encounter on this trip to places of the past?

B. How would they look? What would they say to you?

Partner Action: Part II

More questions to ask:

A. How would you make sure to meet the people of the lands you visit so that you avoid the tourist game of hurried sightseer?

What great things would happen to you with these people?

B. What adventures would you have with the friends you took along on the trip?

C. What would be the outstanding adventure of your whole trip?

ALSO A GROUP GAME

A FANTASY CHALLENGE GAME

This is a game for experienced fantasy players—those who have played a number of games and enjoyed it. The Fantasy Challenge game is not recommended for those who are just beginning their acquaintance with this type of game playing. For advanced players this is a very fast-moving fun game.

Background

The objective of the game is to challenge your partner's creative ingenuity through the introduction of

new elements
new themes
the fabrication of various dilemmas.

A three-minute egg timer is recommended so that each partner can develop his fantasy for a full three minutes or for one and one-half minutes. (Make a mark on the egg timer dividing the white sand in half. Egg timers are available for a small sum at most variety stores.) Determine through trial and error if the longer or shorter fantasy time suits you best. Use of such a timing device is essential for the full enjoyment of the game. It also minimizes the chance of errors in "calling time."

Outline: Part I

Partners begin by agreeing on the general type of fantasy they would both like to have. Should it be a

Travel fantasy
Romance or love fantasy
Science fiction fantasy
Fairy tale fantasy
Action fantasy in the here-and-now?

Choose the type of fantasy that appeals to both of you.

Outline: Part II

Flip a coin. The winner begins the fantasy and has one and one-half or three minutes to develop it. The winner in this case is the hero of his fantasy. The objective of the partner is to introduce new themes or dilemmas which the central character must solve.

For example, Charles B. and Frank L. agreed on an action fantasy in the here-and-now. Charles B. won the toss of the coin.

> He told of winning the Irish Sweepstakes and of buying a specially built race car. He then said he won a number of races and was widely acclaimed by friends and relatives due to this unexpected talent. Charles concluded: "This race made me national champion."

At this point his time ran out and his game partner, Frank L. took over:

> "But not satisfied with this triumph you entered one more race for a minor trophy. Your girl friend Judy was there and she warned you and pleaded with you before the take-off." Frank L. then described the race, Charles' crash and hospitalization. He said "After many operations, you were as good as new, but the doctors and hospital bills had eaten up the remainder of your fortune."

At this point Frank's time ran out and it was now up to Charles to recoup his fortunes and to extricate himself from this dilemma.

Outline: Part III

It is best to agree to put a time limit on this game beforehand. The game is for mutual enjoyment and offers an outstanding opportunity to develop more ingenuity and creativity.

For Group Use

Use it only after the group has played quite a few fantasy games. The host should ask for volunteers who wish to be the central character for the game. The central character holds the egg timer in his hands to time himself. Group members who wish to add to the fantasy raise their hands when time is up to indicate they are ready to add to the fantasy. The central character then picks a volunteer to add his part to the fantasy. (Marking the egg timer at one and one-half minutes makes for a faster pace.)

THE TREASURE HUNT INHERITANCE

This fantasy offers you an opportunity to receive an inheritance and participate in a treasure hunt. This can be an exciting adventure. You can do it very quickly or take a longer time.

Background

You have just now received news of an inheritance. An attorney has phoned you. A distant relative of yours has died and left you the sum of $100,000 (after taxes have been deducted). However, this relative was a little peculiar. He always wanted to go on a treasure hunt; therefore, as his favorite relative, he has specified *that you must spend every penny of this money on a treasure hunt.*

Outline: Part I

You must satisfy his attorney that all the money is spent in pursuing a treasure and not on frills, presents or unrelated things. The attorney will give you the sum in $10,000 installments and you will have to account for how you have spent each $10,000 before you get the next installment.

Outline: Part II

You have just been handed your first $10,000 installment. Here are some questions you may wish to ask yourself (share the answers with your partner):

A. What treasure would you hunt?

B. How would you do it?

C. Can you make up some kind of budget to detail how you would spend your first $10,000?

D. When you have spent it, how about the next $10,000? (and so on)

Outline: Part III

To spend all the money, you may have to seek treasure in various parts of the world.

What treasure would you seek?
How would you do it?

Partners can plan their treasure hunts separately, or can work on this together. It is also fun to involve friends and acquaintances in this game. Get their advice and suggestions.

BECOME AS CHILDREN AND PARENTS FANTASY

This is an action fantasy game for those who would enjoy being either a child or a parent. There is real delight and fun in being a child once more—there are also great satisfactions in being the parent to a child. This duo-game offers you an opportunity to experience both states of being and becoming. It can be played either outside or indoors.

Background

The objective of the game is to become a child, or a parent, if you wish. Be a child, talk as a child, act as a child. Be a parent, talk as a parent and act as a parent. Flip a coin to determine whether you or your partner will be parent or child.

Outline: Part I

Decide what kind of a child or parent you would like to be (see charts below for suggestions). *Don't tell your partner of your choice* (except your age, if a child).

Child Chart:

Age: Below 4
4 to 6
6 to 10
10 to 14
Over

Characteristics:
Spirited, lively
Quiet, calm
Brattish
Curious
Loving, sweet
or   A combination of the above

Parent Chart:

Characteristics:
Indulgent
Stern
Indifferent
Cold
Loving, warm
Happy
or   A combination of the above.

Outline: Part II

Build this fantasy. You are on an outing together. Where are you?

At the circus?
At the beach?
At a boat race?
Shopping?
At a restaurant?
At a concert?
At a play?
At a museum?
At a horse race?

Make up your own outing. (You could actually go to one of these places or do it in fantasy.)

Relate as a parent and a child.

For the Parent:

Be sure to explain things and tell stories if the child is of a certain age.

For the Child:

Be sure to ask the parent for candy, food, drink and other goodies!

REMEMBER, as a parent and child you are on an outing which you both enjoy. The parent can suggest things to do that might be fun for the child, and if the child is in the mood, vice versa.

Outline: Part III (Optional)

Turn about is fair play. The parent can become the child and the child the parent.

THE FAR OUT FANTASY

You are offered a chance to live and experience in fantasy something "far out," something "outlandish." This may be something you have wanted to do or say in your family circle, at home, at work or with friends. It may also be something you have wanted to do when you are alone, or with people.

Background

The objective of the game is to share with your partner something you would have liked to do or say but which you have refrained from doing because others might consider you "too far out." For example:

> People in a park on a hot summer day often have fantasies about jumping into a fountain. Even if they wore shorts or summer clothes, lived close by and were not breaking a law—most people would not do it. They would consider this "far out behavior."

Outline: Part I

Ask yourself the following key question:

> "What is it I have often wanted to do which I consider far out and which I therefore am not doing for many reasons?"

Other examples of far out things people have wanted to do:

> "Wear a kooky outfit."
> "Get a wig or beard." (Color?)
> "Go skinny-dipping in the ocean."

After you have answered the key question, give your partner a turn and let him answer it.

Outline: Part II

What have you wanted to say (or do) to friends or to the family which is far out and which, for various reasons, you have refrained from saying (or doing)?

Examples from fantasy game players:

> *Jack:* (Describes a usual evening meal with family and the personality of the people present.) "Then when everybody is in the middle of the meal I would like to tell them—this scene reminds me of a day at the races, the way we hurry dinner."

> *Carl:* "For some reason I never dared to say this to her—but Carol is a flower."

> *Jane:* "Whenever I am at Jim's place I have ideas how to brighten it up and make it jump. I never told him" (describes).

> *Mary:* (Describes the usual staid organization meeting.) "Right in the middle when they are droning away on 'new business,' I want to jump up and say brightly, 'this is for all of you being such good listeners,' and give everyone an all-day lollipop to suck."

Outline: Part III

What is it you have always wanted to do while at work but for obvious reasons have never done?

Examples:

> *Don:* (Describes office and people in it.) "Just before the mid-morning break I would open that bag I brought with me and quickly let out the six white mice in it. Since this is the busiest time of the day nobody would notice until after the break."

> *Carol:* (Describes Mr. Springer's personality.) "I would like to tell Mr. Springer, who's in charge, that I often think of him as an explorer in Africa, complete with sun helmet and gun. Unfortunately he misses the lion and gets eaten. But then the hyenas sing a beautiful burial hymn, as he lies there a-moldering."

> *Jim:* "She's a very wonderful person and I've thought about presenting her with a bouquet of flowers inscribed 'from all of us at the office.'"

Now let your partner have his turn.

Outline: Part IV

Share with your partner the furthest out thing you have ever done.

THE MOST BEAUTIFUL FANTASY

This is usually a short, very positive fantasy experience. However, some participants find this game so enjoyable they play it for a longer period of time than other fantasy games.

Background

Everyone has a sense of the beautiful and man's aesthetic capacities are among his most treasured gifts. Our sense of the beautiful, just as many of our other powers and abilities, can be developed and extended by deliberately seeking out and cultivating beauty. This fantasy encounter game can serve to deepen both our awareness and range of what we consider aesthetically pleasing and can sharpen aesthetic perception. Our increased awareness of beauty can help us to become more aware of the beauty in us.

Outline: Part I

This game seems to work best if both participants close their eyes during the experience. Participants should also feel free to draw on their past—what they have seen personally or through their experience with exhibits, illustrations, films, and the like.

Begin by picking one of the following:

A. The most beautiful scene in nature which you can create in fantasy.

B. The most beautiful house you can create.

C. The most beautiful garden or park you can shape.

D. The most beautiful clothes for yourself or others.

.Partner Action

The partner can take turns selecting one of the items from the above list if he wishes a more intensive interaction. If you are in the mood for a more quiet experience, let each partner shape and follow his fantasy stream choosing all those items from the above list he wishes to select. Only then take turns.

Outline: Part II

Using fantasy, build the most beautiful society.
What would it *look* like?

DO NOT READ BEYOND THIS POINT. LET YOUR PARTNER'S ACTION BRING YOU THE SURPRISE OF NEW ADVENTURE.

Partner Action: Part I

A. *(Nature scene)* Would you add animals to the nature scene?
Which animals?
What would they be doing?
Now that you have finished creating your fantasy nature scene, would you be interested in introducing a change of seasons?

B. *(House)* Would nature, plants or flowers play a part in the most beautiful house which you are creating?
Would you include a fountain or patio?

C. *(Park)* What unusual (other) features would you include in your garden or park?
How about birds or animals? Sculpture?

D. *(Clothes)* Would you add jewelry or ornaments?

Partner Action: Part II

A. What provision is there in the most beautiful society for nature, for animals and flowers?

B. How would you beautify *one city or town you know,* assuming there are limitless resources at your disposal?

PERSONAL FANTASY COMMUNICATION

It is a very interesting experience, when you are with another person, to share your fantasies about him. Not only is this an enjoyable activity but sometimes you are offered clues to possibilities hidden within circumstances, situations or people.

Background

This experience seems to work best after partners have played a number of fantasy games together. It is helpful if you know your partner fairly well but also works if you are relative strangers to each other.

Outline: Part I

Instructions are simple. Look at your partner, then if you wish, close your eyes and ask yourself this question:

"What potentials or possibilities are hidden within him—what could he do?"

Think about this but do not reveal your answer to your partner; go on to the specific questions contained in Part II.

Outline: Part II

You may now wish to look at the following list of questions and share with your partner the fantasies you have about him related to each question:

1. What are his hidden talents or powers? (What is he capable of doing?)

2. If he had large resources at his command, what do you see him doing?

3. If he were to take a trip, where would it be?

4. If he could change his living environment in any way he chooses, what would his new home look like?

5. If you were to fantasize your partner as a non-human object, what would he be?

6. What do you see happening to your partner in the next five years of his life?

Feel free to make your answer to each question as short or as long as you wish. For an added dimension of experience, have your partner close his eyes so he can let images drift across his mind while you present your fantasies to him using the above list of questions as a guideline.

There is only one ground rule:

DO NOT ATTEMPT TO ANALYZE OR "PLAY PSYCHIATRIST" ON THE BASIS OF THESE FANTASIES.

Let the fantasies be sufficient unto themselves with the focus on a communication experience rich in imagery.

For example, here is part of Dick's personal fantasy communication directed to Jessica:

1. "I see you have *hidden talents* as a dancer or writer. Maybe both. I see you dancing a type of belly dance before a huge audience. But it's not hoochey-koochey, it's your own type of improvised dance form. You are dressed in something almost see-through. Very gossamer veils. Then I see you writing a screenplay. You are at the typewriter, etc."

2. "When you have *a lot of resources and money* I see you directing your own screenplay. You are sitting in the director's or maybe producer's chair looking very happy and busy. Everybody on the set is with it. . . ."

3. "There you are on the deck of a boat *taking a trip* around the world. A full moon is out and you can see the flying fish. Guess who is standing beside you?"

4. "My fantasy about your *new house*—a smallish white palace in Moorish style with a courtyard and waterfall. It's located on a cliff overlooking the ocean. There is a sandy beach. The little palace has five bedrooms. . . ."

5. "As a nonhuman object, I fantasize you as a swift white-maned Arabian horse running freely through the open spaces. . . ."

6. *"In the next five years of your life, you will change jobs and become the head of your own agency. Many people will consult you. You will win a first prize with your first ad campaign. . . ."*

It is particularly important for this experience that you put no fetters on your imagination and that you share with your partner any images or thoughts you might have, however wild they may seem. The objective is to let your fantasy go, go, go.

The best gift to your partner is the free sharing of your fantasies.

THE FEARFUL FANTASY

Almost everyone at some time or another enjoys an excursion into the land of fear and horror and monstrous happenings. It is the purpose of the fearful fantasy to furnish participants with a fantasy adventure into this netherland of imagination.

Background

Objective of the fantasy is to create a feeling of fear and/or horror through use of the imagination. As a part of your fantasy try to create a mood of suspense. If you want to be theatrical, talk like a monster, hiss like a ghost or snarl like a killer. Take your partner to dark places (cemetary or the like), if this is part of your fantasy, thus creating a mood.

Outline: Part I

As you walk along on a street downtown, you will encounter several "environmental triggers." The following is a list of such environmental triggers for this fantasy game:

A policeman
A police car
A fire station
An old house
An undertaker's or funeral-home sign
An ambulance or hearse
A church
A cross
A person dressed in black

Outline: Part II

As soon as you see one of these environmental triggers, the person who has a first turn must tell a fearful fantasy tale involving the trigger. A fearful fantasy may be of the following nature:

A murder fantasy
A horror fantasy
A monster fantasy (involving your favorite monster)
A mystery fantasy
A supernatural fantasy

For example, Frank shared the following supernatural fantasy when he saw a thin and intense looking woman dressed in black (this was his invironmental trigger):

"There is in this city a breed of human vampires which walks among us unnoticed. Sometimes they are dressed in black. The peculiar thing about these vampires is that in addition to sucking blood, they are psychic vampires and fatten on the life energies of people. Have you ever felt completely fatigued and drained? You didn't know it, but a vampire had probably sucked your life energy. Of course these vampires enjoy blood, but blood is to them like caviar is to us. It's a great delicacy which they can't afford very frequently, because otherwise attention would be drawn to them. Well, one night these vampires called a meeting to discuss how they could transform more people into their own kind. . . ."

Outline: Part III

For added excitement, you might wish to use the first person form, i.e. you are the central person in the mystery or supernatural fantasy. You can also involve your partner in the fantasy.

For example,

"Then they caught me and turned me into a vampire. I decided that on a certain night I would have the caviar of your blood. This is the night!" (Frank pounces on his date making her feel fearful.)

If you like, you can see which one of you produces the most fearsome tale and who can send the most chills down the other's back.

THE PARADISE FANTASY

The concept of a paradise can be found in the mythology and theology of many cultures. Most children, if they have not been told about the idea of a paradise by an adult, nevertheless proceed to construct a paradise of their own in fantasy and imagination at some point during the process of growing up. This game offers a delightful experience in building your own paradise.

Outline: Part I

We can call paradise *our own most enjoyable world and how we would have it*. Paradise is very simply the most wonderful world we can create. For example:

> "My paradise is a castle where sumptous banquets can be served at a moment's notice. There is a 'copter at my disposal and I can fly anywhere I want to. The castle/paradise has a large tropical environment under glass. . . ."

Close your eyes and begin to create your paradise.

Outline: Part II

To help out in the process of creation, ask yourself these questions:

What would my paradise look like?
Where would it be?
Who would be in it?
What would be the essential ingredients of my paradise?

DO NOT READ BEYOND THIS POINT. LET YOUR PARTNER'S ACTION BRING YOU THE SURPRISE OF NEW ADVENTURE.

Partner Action: Part I and II

A. Encourage your partner by asking specific questions which help him to go into greater detail about the paradise he is creating. For example, if his paradise includes a dwelling, ask him how it looks from a distance, how many rooms it has, how they are furnished and so on.

B. After your partner has created his paradise in considerable detail, ask him, "How would you spend your first day in your paradise—what would you do?"

PARTNER ACTION

THE PLOT-LINE ACTION FANTASY

This fantasy offers an opportunity for fast-moving fun and action. The game can be played indoors or outdoors and can be of short or long duration. It is recommended for advanced players of fantasy games—those who have played several games and enjoyed them.

Background

You and your partner begin by developing a plot line with both of you as the two central characters. A plot line is simply an outline of a story or probable happening. (See examples below.)

Outline: Part I

A sample of a plot line was worked out by a couple, Tim and Anna. Tim summarized the plot line as follows:

"You and I are explorers in deep jungle country in Africa. We are surrounded by hostile tribes. Most of the animals ignore us for they have never seen human beings. We are looking for a treasure supposed to be hidden in this remote wild country. Eventually we will probably find it. There will be many adventures along the way."

With this plot line as a guide, the couple had an exciting evening. Anna made the following comments about their fantasy adventure after it was over:

"We really had fun fantasizing we were explorers. We managed to get away from the main part of town, walking, and really got lost for a while. This gave us the feeling we were really lost in the jungle. People were animals to us and this was fun. Some people walked like a rhinoceros, others like a giraffe, and so on. A big truck became an elephant. We saw some people in uniform—they were a hostile tribe. When we got hungry, we ordered some exotic dishes at a Chinese restaurant and this was a Chinese trader for us. . . ."

Draw your plot line from any source such as

Fairy tales: for example, you are a folk hero and have adventures, or you are a magician and make things happen.

Movies or plays: pick a film or play one or both of you has seen. Be one of the main characters, or the person playing a smaller role.

News topics: pick your own and be the central person in an event. (Begin by buying a paper.)

Television: select one program, then choose the character you want to play.

Science fiction: use a pocketbook or story in a magazine at a newsstand. Then pick your character.

Play this plot-line action game with one partner carrying out a plot line for a period until it ends. Then it is the other partner's turn.

Outline: Part II

Some partners like to have a series of plot-line action fantasies. They finish with one plot line rather quickly and then start on another. Other partners prefer to spend all evening with one plot line using imaginative dialogue or entering the fantasy when they feel like it. This type of action fantasy can be sustained without pause by being "in and out of character" all evening. Another alternative is dipping in and out of the fantasy as you feel the urge. When it is enjoyable, simply assume the fantasy character you have chosen.

Outline: Part III

By purchasing simple symbolic gifts, your involvement in the fantasy can be deepened. For example, the couple who used the explorer plot line bought candy bars for each other during their respective fantasies. To her, the candy bar was a tropical fruit which she found and shared with him. To him, the candy bar he subsequently bought was a delicious piece of roast meat from an animal he had shot and killed.

The possibilities for plot-line action fantasies are as unlimited as your imagination. You can weave action involving food, drink and symbolic gifts into your fantasy as you chose.

DO NOT READ BEYOND THIS POINT. LET YOUR PARTNER'S ACTION BRING YOU THE SURPRISE OF NEW ADVENTURE.

Partner Action: Parts I, II, III

A. Help your partner select a source from which to fashion a plot line or help him to create his own plot line using his imagination.

B. You may wish to suggest to your partner that you could enter into his fantasy by playing some aspect of his fantasy. (Remember, the intent is to help him along with his fantasy, *not* to introduce new themes or action.)

C. At an appropriate moment give him a symbolic gift and weave it into his fantasy. For example (hand partner an apple): "The visitor from outer space handed him a device, a time machine. He could go back in time for as long as it would take a person to eat an apple."

THE DISASTER SURVIVAL FANTASY

Here is an opportunity to change the world in which we live into a world you would like it to be and have fun while doing it. All the resources in the environment in which you live will be at your command. This is an exciting adventure of reshaping your immediate and larger world.

Background

A major disaster has struck your part of the world. You survive, with a band of others whom you select. You are elected as the person in charge and you have a chance to reshape and rebuild your environment.

The objective of this game is for you and your partner to use ingenuity and imagination after a disaster to create a different type of world from the one we now inhabit.

Outline: Part I

Decide what type of disaster strikes your environment.

Will it be the short-lived but lethal fallout from an H-bomb or A-bomb?

Will it be a biological warfare weapon to which you and other survivors are immune?

Is it a type of ray from the far reaches of the universe that puts almost everyone into a state of hibernation or suspended animation for a period of ten years?; will they then wake up without having aged?

Remember: The rest of the world has been similarly affected and you can hope for no rescue mission from other nations.

Now select a specific disaster.

Describe what happened in detail. Talk about which of your friends, acquaintances and family survived and stayed active.

Outline: Part II

You now have a world at your disposal with almost all facilities intact—but almost completely depopulated. Survivors are looking to you for leadership and suggestions.

A. Where would you live?
How does the place look?
Where is it located?
Where would the other survivors live?

B. What would you do?
Would you "govern?"
What are the first and most important changes you would bring about?

Outline: Part III

Look ahead for ten years. What would be your long-range plans to make this a better world?

DO NOT READ BEYOND THIS POINT. LET YOUR PARTNER'S ACTION BRING YOU THE SURPRISE OF NEW AND EXCITING ADVENTURES.

Partner Action: Part I

A. Tell your partner that a new band of survivors has been added to the original group (go into detail).

B. An accident decimates key people in the original band.

Partner Action: Part II

A. Add to the fantasy by telling your partner that the new band of survivors has people in it who challenge the emerging new way of life.

B. Ask these questions or add your own answers.
How would utilities be provided, communication be maintained?
What arts would be fostered?
How would your group protect priceless art treasures in museums, and so on?

Partner Action: Part III

A. What about the animals—are they turning wild in the abandoned countryside?

B. What are the long-range plans to contact survivors in other nations? What will happen?

For Group Use

The group becomes the band of survivors. The host takes the role of the partner and injects additional action into the progressive group fantasy as indicated.

It is best for the host to indicate the type of disaster which has happened. The group is meeting for the first time immediately after the disaster. The environment is the location (and town or the like) where the group is meeting.

FANTASY ROLES

Be anyone you want to be! This is a fantasy game which can occupy a short period of time or stretch over an entire evening, depending on your mood and enjoyment. It is a *walking game* and can be played while ambling through the streets of a town.

Background

The objective of the game is to carry on with the usual evening activities while seeing the world through the eyes of a person unlike you and *becoming this person.* Be anyone you want to be.

Outline: Part I

Begin the game by picking the person you want to be from the following list (or add to it with your own choices):

Actor, actress
Artist
Cowboy
Intellectual
Anti-intellectual
Swinger
Hippie

Executive type
Grey flannel suit type
Doctor
Airline pilot
Add your own

Outline: Part II

Your partner should now pick someone he wants to be for this game either from the list or make up his own. Help each other choose a role that would be fun to play.

Outline: Part III

Now begin by seeing the world through the eyes of the person you have chosen to be.

How would he talk?
What would he say?
How would he carry himself?
How would he move?
What would be his mannerisms?

As much as you wish to, become that person by talking the way he talks, using his mannerisms, vocalizing his observations about people, and so on. Feel free to "fall out of role," to be your natural self whenever you wish.

Relate to each other as the person you have chosen to be.

For example, be an actress and tell your partner, the cowboy, all about your career, the smashing success of your play and so on. In the meantime he will be entertaining you with stories from his ranch in Texas. You don't have to mimic speech mannerisms if you don't want to—just talk straight.

Outline: Part IV

You can add another dimension of fun and make things more complicated by not telling your partner who you have chosen to be. *Let him guess who you are.* (Perhaps this is for the next time you play this game.)

**PARTNER ACTION
ALSO A GROUP GAME**

THE AMERICAN INDIAN AND AMERICAN GHETTO FANTASY

Many people today are aware of the plight of the American Indian and the economically deprived in our ghettos. Few have let themselves enter into some of the dimensions of feelings these people have or into their life space. This fantasy experience offers such an opportunity and is quite effective in a group.

Background

Some preparation may be necessary for the fantasy experience unless the participant is familiar with the physical setting of an American Indian reservation in the West or has first-hand knowledge of a ghetto/slum area. It is helpful to acquire first-hand knowledge either via an actual acquaintance with the physical environment or by looking at photos, documentary films, television programs and reading recent articles about such an environment.

Outline: Part I

Select whether you will be an American Indian or ghetto inhabitant for the fantasy trip.

Who are you?
Are you married, single, have a family?

Imagine that you are talking to a newspaperman (your partner) who is sympathetic to you and friendly. Use the first person and start talking about yourself. Begin by describing:

A. How you are dressed.

B. When you have last eaten.

C. What you have last eaten.

D. Your physical environment or lifespace—your reservation, your block or your turf.

E. Describe the place where you live in as much detail as possible.

How do you as an Indian/ghetto dweller *feel?*

About those around you
About outsiders
About the government
About welfare workers
About police
About yourself

Outline: Part II

Explore the following:

What do you see as your major problem(s) in life?
How do you feel about organized militant minority organizations such as the Black Panthers?
How do you feel about people drinking, using drugs?

Outline: Part III

Talk about what people or the government could do to help you help yourself.

DO NOT READ BEYOND THIS POINT. LET YOUR
PARTNER'S ACTION BRING YOU THE SURPRISE
OF NEW ADVENTURE.

Partner Action: Parts I, II, III

Your role as the *friendly journalist* or freelance writer is to

listen carefully, and ask encouraging, probing questions (see Part II) which will help clarify the picture that is emerging. Remember you are very interested and you are trying to understand this person and his viewpoint. (Be sure to introduce yourself as a journalist.)

For Group Use

Ask someone (or two persons) to volunteer as members of a minority group or as ghetto inhabitants for a press conference on "Crisis in the Ghetto." Other members of the group are then members of the press corps and ask questions.

For added realism ask for a television crew (simulate mike and equipment).

"Photographers" can ask subjects to pose during press conference.

THE GROOVING RECALL

This game offers an opportunity for a fantastic and enjoyable journey into the past as well as a fantasy in the here-and-now involving people you knew then and people you know now. The game is especially effective if your partner is acquainted with people from your past. However, this game also works if your partner has known you only a short time and knows little or nothing about you.

Background

Each partner should take five minutes and think of people in his life whom he has known well. These can be friends, acquaintances or relatives. (If possible pick people whom your partner knows.)

The objective of the game is to recall instances when people you have known were really grooving:

when they were enjoying life, having a grand time, having a ball.

Outline: Part I

What moments of great joy and happiness do you recall in the lives of these persons you have chosen—moments of great pleasure?

For each person select what you consider the happiest such moment (the time you saw them most joyful).

Begin by describing something of the background of the event.

Describe each incident in as much detail as possible.
What did they do?
How did they react?

Outline: Part II

Now use your fantasy and construct a happy moment for them in the here-and-now.

What incident or experience would bring great happiness to the person today? Describe it in detail. (If your partner does not know the person, describe your relationship to him and give as much background as possible for a fuller understanding of the groovy moment.)

Outline: Part III

Next, share with your partner the grooviest, happiest experience you have had in your life.

Finally, let your partner make up a fantasy.

Let him fantasize *what would be the grooviest experience for you NOW, today.*

THE FANTASY SURPRISE

This is a short, exciting fantasy game. It can be played many times using different settings and surprises.

Background

The object of this game is to build an imagined environment filled with details and people, *in which you as the player are the central figure who gives an imagined gift to your partner, the other central figure.*

Outline: Part I

Build a fantasy story filled with surprises and excitement, leading up to the presentation of a gift or some other positive surprise happening involving your partner. The background for the fantasy surprise can be sketched in very quickly. If you choose a medieval setting, you could say:

"We are in the Middle Ages, in a castle, which I own."

More time can then be spent on the setting and details leading up to the surprise gift.

For example, John's fantasy surprise for Eleanor combined both an event and a gift:

"I've already described the interior hall of the beautiful castle and the dresses of the nobility. As liege lord, I occupy the central position on a throne in the middle of the great hall. We are looking down a long, red carpet towards a door at the other end, through which you will enter for the presentation. Many trumpets sound. A door opens and you slowly enter. You are dressed so beautifully, a murmur of surprise sweeps the room. (Describes her dress and jewelry.) As you slowly advance toward me, ten small children in gorgeous velvet outfits suddenly appear to strew flowers in your path. The orchestra plays beautiful music. Finally I reach behind me, into the jewelry casket, and bring out an exquisite diadem, or small crown, as a token of your nobility. Then I read a scroll which says. . . ."

When it was her turn, Eleanor placed John on a South Sea desert island where he was marooned and lonely. The fantasy surprise was her appearance after a stormy shipwreck, from which she had fortuitously escaped.

The fantasy surprise game has an infinite number of possibilities and settings in which the two central figures present positive surprises to each other after much adventure and happenings. It can be an exciting and happy fantasy game.

ANIMAL PERSONIFICATION FANTASY

This is an experience which can be a lot of fun if you are walking in a park on an evening or if you are in a part of town where there is relative privacy. Slight variations of this game can be played on a busy street, or indoors. This can be either a short or long fantasy experience.

Background

The object of this game is to enter a fantasy, experiencing and seeing the world through the eyes of the animal you select to be; then you share your fantasies. It is the play experience of being an animal in your imagination.

Outline: Part I

Select the animal you would like to be for this game from the following list, or choose any other animal you would especially like to be:

Cat
Tiger
Horse
Bear
Lion
Deer
Monkey
Gorilla
Cheetah
Etc.

Outline: Part II

A. Now, *be* that animal. See the world through its eyes. Imagine the park or city as a jungle. If you are in a park, begin to move like that animal, make the noises of that animal. Imagine you are that animal in human form, that by some magic you have become transformed to match that animal's style.

B. If you are on a busy street, stop frequently and, unobserved, make the small, unobtrusive movements of that animal. You can change your style of walking to some degree to resemble the animal's style of locomotive. Use varied head movements, smooth your fur, flex your claws, and so on.

C. You can take turns or you can both be the animals of your choice at the same time. Remember, you will move like that animal.

Adapt your communication in some ways to be like that of your animal choice, and so on. Play this way for five or ten minutes.

D. Now *share a fantasy of what that animal was doing as it was moving through the jungle, woods, or whatever.*

Outline: Part III (Optional)

For an added dimension of excitement, don't tell your partner what animal you have chosen to be. Let him guess. Don't give too many clues too early. Every five or ten minutes in the midst of your conversation, give your partner a subtle hint by briefly assuming some mannerism or vocal quality of the animal you have chosen to be.

THE MYSTERY FANTASY GAME

Mysteries have always had a certain charm and attraction. They intrigue us and make us curious. Perhaps one of the attractions of a mystery is that it gives us a chance to play. We let our imaginations play with the alternative possibilities inherent in the mystery. The mystery fantasy game combines the elements of mystery, play and imagination and presents participants with a multitude of frameworks for experiencing the unknown.

This is a game for advanced players—those who have played a number of fantasy encounter games and enjoyed them.

Background

The purpose of the game is to instill feelings of mystery and suspense in the player and partner and to keep these feelings on a high level as the game unfolds. Some advance preparation for the game is necessary. A three-minute, hour-glass-type egg timer is needed.

As soon as the player has been chosen, the partner in the game should copy each statement on pages 77-78 called "mystery happenings" on a separate slip of paper. These action slips should then be placed face down so that the players can draw one at the end of each three minutes.

The egg timer should be placed outside of the line of vision of the player so that he cannot watch his time. When three minutes are up, the partner signals by holding up his hand. At this time the player must draw an action slip and incorporate what is written on the slip in his developing fantasy. Duration of this fantasy game is usually limited to three or four action slips. *Wristwatches of both player and partner should be taken off: otherwise, nervous clock watching is encouraged.*

Three elements of suspense are present in this game: the suspense of the developing fantasy, the suspense of time and that added by the action slips. The main focus of the player should be on having fun and creating as suspenseful a fantasy as he can.

Outline: Part I

There are many possibilities for the creation of a suspenseful, mysterious fantasy. What type do you prefer?

> Ghost fantasy
> Science fiction fantasy
> Fairy-story fantasy
> Detective or murder fantasy
> Adventure fantasy

Choose the type that would be most fun to play with and to develop. (If you want to, take a few minutes and, using key words, outline or jot down the major points or series of incidents in the fantasy you have selected.) Many players, however, seem to enjoy the spontaneous unfolding of the story as they go along and prefer not to use an outline. Decide if you will use the first person or third person while telling this fantasy.

Outline: Part II

Begin by describing the initial setting or environment in which the mystery fantasy begins:

A house,
Woods,
Rocket ship,
Where?

Be detailed in your description.

Now describe the central character.

If you do a first-person fantasy begin, for example, by saying:

"I am a detective, stockily built, in my early twenties. . . ."

If third person, give a detailed description of your central character.

Proceed with your mysterious, suspenseful fantasy, but remember, when three minutes are up your partner will hold up his hand. This is the time for you to draw an action slip and incorporate' what is written on the slip in your ongoing fantasy.

DO NOT READ BEYOND THIS POINT. LET YOUR PARTNER'S ACTION BRING YOU THE SURPRISE OF NEW ADVENTURE.

Partner Action

Before the game begins, copy each item on the list of mystery happenings on a separate slip of paper. Place these action slips face down on a table or let your partner draw an action slip in such a way that he cannot see what is written on it.

List of Mystery Happenings

A. There is a joyous festival

B. A ghost or monster appears

C. Central character falls in love

D. An act of God intervenes—tornado, earthquake, thunderstorm or the like

E. A happy reunion

F. A murder or accident

G. Central character meets the president of the United States

H. A journey to the U.S.S.R. or Asia

I. Someone is born

J. An act of caring or love or great kindness

K. Add your own mystery happenings (limit to two additional action slips)

THE OUT OF SIGHT FANTASY

This fantasy game is for a day or evening when you are feeling in a far-out mood, when you feel capricious or daring and eager to try new flights of the imagination. This can be either a slow-moving or a fast-paced fantasy experience. It is a good group game if many of the people know each other well.

Background

The objective of the game is to imagine circumstances, actions, environments or happenings *which are designed to amaze and astonish the people you know*. Ask yourself this question:

"What circumstance, experience or incident would result in the utter astonishment, amazement and possibly attitude change and personal growth in my friend (or friends)?"

Outline: Part I

Begin by selecting someone known to you and your partner. This may be a friend, an acquaintance or a member of your family.

Outline: Part II

Now imagine an incident, experience or happening that he would never conceive of, that he would consider "out-of-sight."

For example one player of this game, Max R., had this flight of fantasy:

"You know our friend Jack who is so shy? It would absolutely flip him if all of us got together, had a surprise party for him and all evening everybody told him how great he was. People would urge him to play the piano. He would be the center of attention. All the girls would be in on this, pay a lot of attention to him and be bold, especially Cindy. At the end of the evening, we would have the group cheer him and give him a trophy of some sort. This would really overwhelm him or make him freak out in a positive way."

Outline: Part III

Partners playing this game can build on each other's fantasies, extend them or even change them. For example, Max

R.'s partner added the following to Max's fantasy about what would amaze Jack:

> "The greatest thing that would surprise Jack is a harem scene. We have three or four fellows dressed as harem guards and servants in the oriental manner. The whole place is transformed into a harem with wall hangings and incense, pillows on the floor, oriental music, and the like. We get all the girls Jack knows; they dress in oriental costumes. The girls take turns feeding him and put on a seduction scene for him. That would do it."

Players can also imagine unexpected happenings for people their opposite partner does not know. *In this case it is necessary to give a short character sketch of the person.* Describe the type of person he is. For example, Max said:

> "My boss is a very uptight person. The type who counts paper clips. He does not drink, is always correctly dressed and is very religious and puritan. Imagine how he would feel—it would blow his mind if *his* boss, the chairman of the board, would call for him to come to his office on the top floor. The office, one of those ultra-modern places with a concealed bar, would be filled with children's toys, obviously played with. The chairman would meet him semi-nude, his hands covered with finger paint and a drink in his hand. His greeting would be 'Come on in. I am relaxing playing with these. Have a drink and let's have a play session. Help me with these finger paints. Boy is this fun.' The boss couldn't say no. He respects the chairman. It would really surprise him."

Depending on the mood or inclination of players the Out-of-Sight Fantasy can be used in relation to a number of people in quick succession, or it can be a leisurely game which extends over the evening. As a conclusion for the game each partner can share *what he imagines would overwhelm or "freak out" his partner*.

For Group Use

This should not become a destructive "put down game" involving members of the group. If participants use this game in a hostile manner against each other, suggest they use only people who are not present for their out-of-sight fantasies.

PARTNER ACTION

FANTASY DIALOGUE WITH SIGNIFICANT OTHERS

"Significant others" are those persons in your life who really matter to you: your parents, grandparents, brothers, sisters and friends. Whether these persons are alive today or not, you can have a fantasy dialogue with them. This can be a very positive experience which can result in new insights and understanding.

Background

For this experience you may want to go back into your past, to recall incidents from your adolescence and childhood. Begin this game by sharing with your partner something of your background. Talk about where you grew up, your parents and other family members, their personalities and physical appearance. Draw a word picture of some of these significant people.

For understandable and complex reasons, all too often persons who matter to us have not been in the position to offer us a large measure of encouragement and support when we desired it. Nevertheless, the overwhelming majority of significant people in our lives have given us support and praise at some time during our association with them. They have probably given to us in this way many times, but we have forgotten. Although we may have forgotten, feeling tones linger and reverberate over long periods of time. This fantasy game can strengthen these good feeling tones, bringing a renewed sense of our relatedness to others and to ourselves.

Outline: Part I

Begin by mentally reviewing the list of significant persons in your life. Ask yourself this question:

> With which two persons did I have the best relationship either as a child or as an adolescent?

Draw a word picture of these two persons. Was it a friend, teacher, relative, neighbor? Share with your partner some of the highlights of your relationship with them.

Outline: Part II

Now select an outstanding achievement on *your part* which has occurred during the past five to ten years. This may be an occasion which no one else has ever known about or noticed, something that gave you a great sense of satisfaction and pride on completion.

Now tell one of the two persons you have selected (Part I) about this achievement or accomplishment. Go into detail. Pretend the person is there with you and address him. You can pretend your partner is the person you have chosen. Or, imagine the person is seated on a chair in front of you.

Outline: Part III

When you have finished telling him about this accomplishment, use your fantasy; *what would this person reply?*

How do you imagine he would have praised, encouraged and supported you?

If you are sitting down, change seats. Try to talk somewhat like this significant person. *Become this person* and address the chair where you were formerly sitting, as he would speak to you.

Outline: Part IV (Optional)

Repeat the whole process with the other person you have selected.

DO NOT READ BEYOND THIS POINT. LET YOUR PARTNER'S ACTION BRING YOU THE SURPRISE OF NEW ADVENTURE.

Partner Action: Part I

A. If your partner has difficulty in identifying the two people with whom he had the best relationship during childhood or adolescence, first encourage him to talk more about these periods. There may be a friend, relative or teacher in the picture that he has forgotten.

B. Should your partner still be unable to identify such a person, tell him to find that person with whom he has had the best relationship over the last five to ten years of his life.

Partner Action: Part II

A. Convey to your partner that he need not be modest with you in taking pleasure in something he has done. Perhaps he could make an effort not to let a false sense of modesty hold him back. Tell him that you would like to hear about his accomplishment and that this is part of the game. Furthermore, the freer he is with you, the freer you can be when your turn comes.

B. Encourage your partner to select something which he has done of which he was really proud or which *filled him with a sense of deep satisfaction.*

Partner Action: Part III

A. When your partner gets ready to become one of the two persons with whom he has had the best relationship, encourage him to change seats; this change of position often facilitates assuming the role of another person.

B. Suggest that after he has changed seats it may help him to become this person by talking with his eyes closed.

PARTNER ACTION

THE EXCITING FANTASY

There is general agreement among social and behavioral scientists that we live in a time of massive social change. This fantasy game gives you a chance to play an important role in bringing to society the type of change *you* feel is best.

Background

Imagine that through a combination of circumstances too complex to detail here, this country has reached the brink of a national crisis and has gone over the brink. The forces unleashed by this crisis have brought home to every American citizen the realization that to survive we must initiate change in our institutional structures, but that *this change must take place within the framework of democratic processes and our Constitution.* State and national congressional and senatorial representatives are now willing to implement the will of the electorate rather than be guided mainly by the special interest groups who have contributed financially to their election. There is a widespread grass-roots movement to initiate social regeneration since *all* segments of society have realized that

the alternatives are:

> change within the democratic framework, or
> chaos and civil war, or
> a repressive dictatorship.

Again, through complex circumstances you have been named *chief expediter of your state.* Your state has been singled out as a model program. Your role as chief expediter is to recommend and bring about institutional change based on the wishes of the electorate. Accordingly you have set up a network of grass-root town meetings all over the state in which the issue of institutional regeneration is explored through dialogue, and recommendations are made. These recommendations are then coded and fed through regional centers into computers so that the intent of the people can be communicated through the media, and further clarification can be undertaken. The country has become an action-oriented, working democracy.

You find that as things have worked out, some of your major ideas for social regeneration have been approved by the people of your state. Your function now as chief expediter is to set change in motion—to initiate institutional regeneration.

Assume that in every municipality you will find a church, a governmental or educational institution ready and eager to become a model or "demonstration agency" geared to total change. This, while the laws are being passed designed to bring about this change. They are looking to you to implement specific ideas, a specific plan.

Outline: Part I

With what institution would you begin the program of regeneration, and *what would you do?* ●

> *Educational*—which level?
> *Church*—which?
> *Government*—local, police, agriculture, health, welfare?
> *Family*—what structures, what change in laws are needed?

Outline: Part II (Optional)

You are suddenly asked to take special responsibility to expedite programs for the

> ghettos
> aged
> American Indian

What model programs would you initiate?
What new legislation would you ask for?
DO NOT READ BEYOND THIS POINT. LET YOUR
PARTNER'S ACTION BRING YOU THE SURPRISE
OF NEW ADVENTURE.

Partner Action: Part I

Assist your partner in picking the two institutions which interest him most in relation to beginning his program of institutional regeneration.

Partner Action: Part II

Help your partner to be as specific as possible—but do it gently, caringly. Assist him in developing his ideas.

> Ask pertinent questions. Point out possible obstacles which need to be overcome. Support your partner in his planning and the implementing of action. Compliment and encourage him if this feels right to you. (You may not agree with all of his suggestions. You can implement your ideas when it is your turn.)

Partner Action: Part III

If you wish, take the role of a member of one (or several) of the programs your partner has decided to expedite.
Imagine you are

> a ghetto member or an American Indian, and you are speaking to the chief expediter, stating *the needs* of your people (not their wishes, but their needs and problems).

Partner's Turn

THE ADVERTISING TRIGGER GAME

This great game involves you more and more as the evening progresses. It is a game to be played when walking through the streets.

Background

Choose one of the main streets downtown for this walking fantasy. As you walk down the street, you see many types of advertisements on billboards, store fronts, street signs and so on. These are used to trigger a journey into the land of imagination and adventure.

Outline: Part I

Begin the game with each partner selecting an advertising category such as:

> Liquor ads (can be subdivided into beer and hard liquor),
> Cigarette ads
> Lingerie ads
> Dairy ads
> Travel ads, etc.

The category you select will be noted by your partner who will then begin to look for this type of ad.

Outline: Part II

Start walking. When you see an ad in your partner's category, point it out. Show him the particular example you have selected and ask him to make up a fantasy—long or short—*using all the words in the advertisement.*

Your fantasy can either be a wildly imaginary tale that comes to an end, or it can be a progressive fantasy that you continue on the next turn, very much like a serial story which you keep on building and shaping.

As Jim and Mary were walking along, he pointed out a trigger sign which read "Grandmammy's Bourbon—The Smoothest and the Best!" (She had selected the hard liquor category of advertisements.) They both stopped briefly and Mary decided she wanted to tell a progressive fantasy and began with the following story:

> "There was this *grandmammy* descended directly from the Royal House of *Bourbon*. Come to think of it, she was fond of bourbon, too. Of all that noble family, she was about *the smoothest operator*. Her cunning *and* intelligence were widely admired. One day she set out to find *the best* suitor for her granddaughter, a beautiful and ravishing girl, tall and green-eyed. . . ." (She used all seven words in the advertisement as a part of her fantasy.)

Outline: Part III

Each partner takes turns. After Mary's turn, she looked for cigarette ads, which Jim had chosen as his category.

Outline: Part IV (Optional)

You can use other signs for this type of fantasy game. For example, you can take turns and pick a sign in window displays of shops such as clothing stores, flower shops, gift shops or the like, and use this as a base for your fantasy. In this case, each partner chooses a different category of shop. The other partner then selects the sign to be used for the fantasy on locating such a shop.

A ground rule is that *all* words in the sign must be used as a part of the advertising trigger game.

THE SEX FANTASY SHARING GAME

Relatively few people ever share their sexual fantasies. Yet, if they do, this can bring a number of positive outcomes. This game offers an opportunity to share such fantasies. It is obviously a game for only the most daring and courageous.

Background

Most people have sexual fantasies several times throughout the day. Many also have the same, or similar, sexual fantasies which recur over a period of time. For the most part, sexual fantasies are enjoyed by those who have them. Perhaps this generates a measure of guilt which some persons experience. At any rate sexual fantasies are rarely communicated.

The sharing of sexual fantasies can bring a new sense of freedom, add new dimensions to communication, and can enhance self-understanding and awareness. The verbal communication and the recognition that everyone has sexual fantasies can also result in the disappearance or lessening of guilt feelings associated with such fantasies. Many people who lead happy and fulfilled sex lives believe they have "far out" or unusual sex fantasies. When these are communicated in a group these people often find that others have very similar fantasies and that theirs are not as unusual as they thought they were.

Since it takes courage to share fantasies and to play fantasy games, and even greater courage to share sex fantasies and to play the Sex Fantasy Sharing Game, this game has been placed at the end of the duo-game section. This game is particularly effective and enjoyable if three to four other games from this and the Sensory Fantasy Game Section are played first. In this particular game, it is best *not* to read ahead but to read *only* PART I, do it, then proceed to read PART II, etc.

Outline: Part I

Begin by sharing what you believe to be the most frequent sexual fantasies of men and women: If you are a man, share with your partner what you believe to be the most frequent sexual fantasy which women have.

If you are a woman, share with your partner what you believe to be the most frequent sexual fantasy which men have.

You should both be as explicit as possible and not restrict yourselves to general statements.

Outline: Part II

Now, *using your life experience and association with people at a base,* if a woman, ask yourself this question: "From conversation and hints picked up, what would appear to be the most frequent sexual fantasies of WOMEN?"

If you are a man, ask yourself this question: "From conversation and hints picked up, what would appear to be the most frequent sexual fantasies of MEN?"

(It may be best to begin PART II by having a three-minute quiet time, with eyes closed, to facilitate recall.)

Be as detailed in response to above questions as you can be.

Outline: Part III

Now flip a coin to determine who is first. Winner now shares his own most frequent sexual fantasy—the sexual fantasy you have most often—whatever it might be, involving man, woman, several people, animals or things.

Remember:

Never feel guilty about fantasying
and sharing your fantasies.

Outline: Part IV

You may now wish to share you reaction to this experience, *how you feel now,* what you have learned about yourself and each other, etc.

If played in a group, divide participants into couples and let them get acquainted. Then slowly read Part I, then Part II, then III. Allow time for completion of each Part. For Part IV have group sit in a circle for a group discussion.

AN INDEX TO WALKING FANTASY ENCOUNTER GAMES

For those who like to do their fantasying out of doors, or while strolling through the streets, the following is a list of Walking Games. These games utilize specific stimuli, or inputs, found outdoors. It is also possible, of course, to play many of the duo-games outdoors while walking, if this is preferred. Some group games, too, have been included in this list of walking games, as they can easily be adapted and played as games for two (duo-games).

SENSORY FANTASY GAMES

The objective of sensory fantasy games is to help you become more aware of your senses and the feel of your body, to become more sensitive to your inner rhythm, your muscles and skin and in the process, to use and develop your imagination and capacity to fantasize.

Some of the sensory fantasy games are for two people; others are designed for a group experience.

Participants can enter into a fantasy of being a slow animal, a fast animal, even a bird, and then a baby once more.

There is a fantasy walk, best taken in a beautiful natural setting, and your imagination is stimulated by an encounter with "fantasy triggers." With the awakening of your sense of touch and smell, common objects in our environment become exciting events. Tasting and eating become an adventure as you experience the joyful eating game.

ALSO A GROUP GAME

THE SENSORY ADVENTURE GAME

This fantasy game is played at home and takes a little advance preparation. One partner can volunteer to make the preparations for the game, or you can surprise your partner by having everything ready.

Background

This game is based on the finding that the smell of herbs and spices and other odors can trigger ideas and fantasies in most people. It can open new doors of sensory awareness and can be fun.

Outline: Part I

To prepare for the game, go to your spice cabinet and select the most aromatic herbs and spices you can find—the more, the better. Such spices and herbs as sage, rosemary, sweet basil, cloves, cinnamon, cardamom, nutmeg and ginger have an especially pleasing smell. If you wish, you can also add some colognes and perfumes, drops of which can be placed on cloth squares or handkerchiefs.

Begin with the herbs and spices. The greater the variety of aromas and fragrances, the better the game will be. Wrap all spice boxes so that the contents cannot be identified. The simplest way is to scotchtape paper around each container. Be sure to conceal the top so that visual identification is impossible. You can also place pieces of orange peel or lemon peel at the bottom of a small paper bag squeezed together to leave an opening for the nose.

Outline: Part II

The object of this game is to free your imagination, to trigger images, to recall and to fantasize. Try not to identify the source of each aroma. Just flow with the experience—take your time—let your mind wander. Let the aromas trigger the free flow of imagination from your inner universe. Share with your partner any images, ideas, and associations that come to mind. Have fun sharing sentence fragments, image fragments, idea fragments, memory fragments. If eyes are closed, a very enjoyable adventure into fantasy and the building of an imagery collage can begin.

Outline: Part III

Take turns smelling the different aromas. Keep your eyes closed while your partner hands aroma containers to you.

Outline: Part IV

After you have each had your turn, part of the fun can be the unveiling and identifying of aromas.

For added enjoyment, if the seasons are right, place a variety of fresh green herbs in small brown bags and crush them slightly. Pine leaves, pine straw and other leaves and flowers can be used effectively.

For Group Use

The host should prepare the odor containers in advance. Stress that there be no identifying of the odor—but that everyone close their eyes and share a fantasy as they wish—*while inhaling the aroma of the container*—as it is passed around.

THE JOYFUL EATING GAME

This game offers the possibilities of a fantasy which you can have in your home or in a restaurant while you are eating breakfast, lunch or dinner. This can be a short experience or can continue throughout the meal.

Background

Your fantasy can be anything you want it to be. It may involve you and your partner in a fantasy situation or it may include only make-believe people. Again the device of progressive fantasy can be used, i.e. you begin an imaginative tale, then your partner continues it and you build on his continuation when your turn comes again. Throughout this you will weave various "fantasy triggers" into the unfolding stream of images and happenings.

Outline: Part I

Establish a timing device first. If you are at home you may wish to play the radio softly while you eat and use the next station break as your "time-is-up" indicator. (Every time there is a station break it is someone's turn.) If you are in a restaurant, people entering or leaving, movements of the waitresses past certain tables and so on may be used to indicate turns.

Outline: Part II

As soon as your turn comes up:

Look at your fork or recall the last bite you have eaten—then weave a fantasy around the food on your fork or the last bite you took.

For example, Mary had a piece of roast beef and potato on her fork (the fantasy trigger) when the announcer cut in; so she made up fantasies about the meat and potato.

"Once there was a beautiful black and white cow that lived in the field of a farmer named Ezekiel. . . ."

and "One day a farmer was working in a potato field in Idaho when he saw an astounding event. . . ."

Fantasies can be quite short (two or three sentences) or as long as you wish. The main objective of the game is to have fun fantasizing while you are eating.

In order to avoid repetition (in Mary's case she may be eating beef again on her next turn) you can also

Make up a fantasy about any object on the table which becomes a fantasy trigger.

If in a restaurant you can make up a fantasy about

People sitting nearby
The waitress or waiter(s)
Parts of the decor of the restaurant.

Outline: Part III (Optional)

As you are sitting there watching your partner eat, have a fantasy about him.
If he were to be food, what sort of food would he be?

Birthday cake?
A sausage?
A Cheese? (What kind?)
A hamburger?

Share this fantasy if you wish.

THE JOLLY DRINKING GAME

This is a very simple and easy fantasy game which can be played either at home, while on a date or in town.

Background

Surprise your partner with something exotic. The objective is for your partner to build a fantasy story around the surprise drink which you present to him. This fantasy story can involve both of you, be a fairy tale, science fiction story or imaginative adventure.

Outline: Part I

There are, for example, a wide variety of alcoholic mixed drinks with exotic names such as the Zombie, Mai-Tai, Green Hornet, Scorpion, Marguerita and Black Russian. There are also a tremendous variety of liqueurs such as Kahlua, Anisette, Creme de Cacao, Creme de Banana, Picon, Pernod, Tia Maria, Chartreuse and Cointreau, as well as the various brandies.

In the nonalcoholic field there is also a tremendous variety. Any drugstore will offer a number of exotic sodas and ice-cream soda combinations which your partner has most likely not tried. Finally, there is a wide selection of tropical fruit juices ranging from passion fruit juice to guava, papaya, apricot, pineapple and pear juice. Many of these are available in supermarkets.

Begin by *choosing a new and different drink for your partner.* Let your partner taste this drink.

> (To add spice to the game ask him to close his eyes while tasting and *do not reveal the identity of the drink.*)

Outline: Part II

Now ask your partner to build a fantasy around

	A.	The taste of the drink
or	B.	The smell of the drink
or	C.	The name of the drink
or	D.	A fantasy on all three

Outline: Part III

Take turns.

Make up your own drinks with any exotic, wild sounding names you wish.

Continue sharing fantasies as in Part II.

Have joy!

INTRODUCTION TO THE ANIMAL GAMES

Animals are not only sources of food, entertainment and delight, but they also have something to teach us. By using our empathy, "getting into the skin of an animal" and its movement rhythm, we can discover and recover elements and harmonies of our own inner rhythmic being. We can also break through to a new "in-touchness" with ourselves by using the rhythms of inanimate objects.

Animal games can be used if you are by yourself but work best in a group. In either case, tape recording the instructions is very helpful, especially since it frees the host to participate in the games.

Instructions which follow for the game sequence may either be read aloud, or you can use your own words. Pauses or silences are indicated. *When reading these instructions aloud, it is very important to allow long silences.* When you think you should break the silence to continue reading, do not do this; allow at least as much time to go by again. The most common complaint for this experience is "You didn't give us enough time to do our thing." Watch the group and give them plenty of time to enjoy themselves.

To begin the sensory fantasy game, wear comfortable clothing (pants or shorts for women). Shoes and socks can be taken off if anyone feels like it. If possible, have this experience in the open, in a beautiful setting. If a room is used, it should be large and carpeted.

THE SLOW ANIMAL GAME

Slowly read the following:

This is an experience of being a slow animal, feeling your way into its body rhythms, and discovering your own in the process. All animal games are a nonverbal experience. Refraining from talking helps us listen to our bodies more closely.

Now close your eyes and ask yourself:

What slow-moving animal you want to be. (PAUSE)

What slow animal has fascinated you? (PAUSE)

Which have you watched again and again as a child or adult? (PAUSE)

Was it a snail? (PAUSE)

A turtle? (PAUSE)

A slow-crawling snake? (PAUSE)

A worm?

Choose the slow animal you'd like to be. (LONG PAUSE)

Begin by getting into the position of the animal. Lie down, squat or do whatever you want to do—but be that animal resting quietly. (PAUSE)

> Feel yourself into the skin of that animal. (PAUSE) Sniff the air; enjoy the sun on your hide while resting, being lazy and contented. (PAUSE)

Now, slowly begin to move. If you meet other animals crawling along, fine. Keep moving. You are friendly, contented, well fed. (LONG PAUSE)

If you wish, change and become another slow-moving animal. Now begin to slow down even more. You are weary and ready to rest a while. (LONG PAUSE)

THE CHOICE ANIMAL GAME

Suppose a magician told you you could be any animal you want to be except a bird. What would you be? (PAUSE)

Would you like to be

> a deer, bear, rabbit, wolf, horse, elephant, giraffe, cow, lynx or cheetah, lion, tiger, fox, dog or cat?

What animal have you watched with fascination? (LONG PAUSE)

Choose the animal you would like to be.

Be that animal and begin to move like that animal. Move along in a friendly way, well fed, sniffing the air, enjoying the scenery and everything. (LONG PAUSE)

Now move a little faster.

Go at a fast pace or trot if you want to. (LONG PAUSE)

You can change and be another animal if you want to. (PAUSE)

Now begin to slow down. If you want to, you can lie down and be that completely relaxed, resting animal. (PAUSE) Enjoy the air, the sun on your hide. Close your eyes if you want to. Enjoy being the animal, resting. (LONG PAUSE)

THE ANIMAL PLAY GAME

Slowly read the following:

Can you remember watching young animals play? You have probably seen puppies, kittens or bear cubs at play. Pick a young animal that you would like to be. (PAUSE)

Ask yourself what young animal you would like to be. (LONG PAUSE)

Growl, or yip like the playful young animal that you are.

Make any animal sound you wish. (PAUSE)

Begin to play by yourself—be that young animal,

playing,

running around,

chasing its tail,

enjoying solitary play.

(LONG PAUSE)

Now, slowly begin to play with a young animal nearby.
Be playful.
Remember, young animals don't hurt each other—play gently. (LONG PAUSE)
All right, a thunderstorm is coming and all the young animals must stop their play.
Please stop and, if you wish to, take a rest. (LONG PAUSE)

THE BIRD GAME

The game will work only if there is plenty of space for the birds to swoop and fly. It is best done outdoors, on the grass.

This is your chance to be a bird!
Play this game silently.
What bird would you like to be?

a hawk, a gull, a swallow, a pigeon, a love-bird, a crane, or a flamingo? (PAUSE) Choose the bird you want to be and be that bird.

First, pretend you are earthbound.

Stand, sit, walk around, bask in the sun, do whatever you feel like—but do not fly. (LONG PAUSE)

Now, shake your wings, look around and do what you usually do to get ready to fly. Your arms are your wings. (PAUSE)

Now, raise your wings, take off and start flying.

Swoop and glide—fly slow or fast. You're flying! (LONG PAUSE)

(Watch the group until a few are beginning to slow down then begin to end the game.) You are now coming down to land.

Are there other birds around you?
How do you feel about yourself?
Did you enjoy flying?

Let's talk about how it feels to be a bird.

THE BE AN OBJECT GAME

Slowly read the following:

This is a fun game. To play it successfully, you must become a child once more. Do you remember as a child playing at being a locomotive, a racing car, a steamboat or a fire engine? (PAUSE)

Choose to be any object that you would like to be, such as

locomotive, racing car, ferris wheel, merry-go-round, rocket, machinery, steamboat. (LONG PAUSE) You can make the sounds of that object.

Now, close your eyes and feel yourself as that object. (PAUSE) Begin to move slowly, the way that object wants to move. (LONG PAUSE) Now go slower and slower and come to a full stop. (LONG PAUSE) Resume your personhood.

THE BABY GAME

This is your chance to be a baby once more, to feel like a baby and to be a baby. (PAUSE)

You can be a baby in a crib joyfully waving his arms and legs about or just resting, or a crawling baby. You can also make the sounds of a baby if you want to. (LONG PAUSE)

Feel yourself into the being of that baby and remain with your eyes closed, at rest. (LONG PAUSE)

Lie there, for a while, like a baby in the crib, before you move around. Feel like the baby feels. Think like the baby and sense like the baby that you are. (LONG PAUSE)

Now be a happy, satisfied baby that has just had a good meal, is feeling content and feels good about himself and the world.

You are a happy, contented, interested baby. (LONG PAUSE)

Slowly begin to explore what it is like to sit up, then to crawl. Do this with eyes closed as much as you can. (LONG PAUSE)

If you feel like it, you can

> play with some of the other babies or just ignore them. Do what you want to do and enjoy it. (LONG PAUSE) Begin to slow down. You are getting a little weary. (PAUSE)

Now begin to close your eyes and rest as a baby. (LONG PAUSE) Now with your eyes closed, slowly begin to grow up until you reach adulthood—a new adulthood which incorporates some of the childlike qualities you have experienced!

THE NONVERBAL GIFT GAME

This group game can be played at home or, if there is a warm, sunny day, on a lawn or in a backyard.

The game works best if at least five to six or more persons are present to participate. It can be used with special effectiveness after everyone has had a chance to become acquainted with each other and after some general interaction or conversation among participants has taken place.

Outline: Part I

Explain the purpose of the game in the following or similar words:

> "Let's play a game called nonverbal gifts. For this game, we need a volunteer who will lie on his back

on the floor with his eyes closed. He will have a very pleasant and caring experience. This is what we will do:

"After the volunteer lies down in the middle of the floor with his eyes closed, we will go up to him *one at a time* and slowly, caringly, give him a nonverbal gift. By nonverbal gift, we mean that there is no talking. We can gift the person by, for example, stroking his hair, gently massaging his hand or foot, putting our hands on his brow. We do this slowly and in a loving, caring manner so that the person will have a very good experience. While this is happening he just relaxes and enjoys the experience, letting his fantasy flow where it may."

Outline: Part II

After everyone has given the person a nonverbal gift, the host can suggest that he sit up. He can then be asked whether he would like to share any fantasies he may have had while being the recipient of the nonverbal gifts. Finally, he can be asked,

"What is your reaction to this experience?" OR "How do you feel now?"

NOTE: If you wish to play this game with a partner, one of you becomes the volunteer, the other gives him a minimum of four nonverbal gifts while he lies on the floor with eyes closed. It is important to *give him nonverbal gifts slowly* and to prolong the giving of each nonverbal gift as long as possible. There should be a period of quiet between each nonverbal gift.

THE COLLAGE FANTASY

A change of pace, the collage fantasy is an enjoyable experience of constructing a visual fantasy, designed for a stay-at-home evening. No advance preparation for the game is needed if glue, scotch tape, scissors and a number of old magazines and newspapers are available. Adding color crayons is helpful. The game is also very effective with a group of people.

Background

The objective of the game is to translate a fantasy into visual imagery and only then to explore the ramifications of the fantasy verbally. A collage can be constructed by pasting or fastening cutouts of illustrations, parts of illustrations, words and phrases on a large piece of paper. The creation of such a construction is in itself a pleasurable and exciting activity.

Outline: Part I

You can either begin by thinking through what type of collage fantasy you want to create or you can "let it grow" i.e. begin with something, add something that seems to fit, then add more, letting it come into being organically.

In the latter case it could become a "non-intellectual trip" by placing major emphasis on following your feelings and intuition as to what to put together. Use your imagination and creativity to produce the fantastic. (Each person creates his own collage.) When you have completed your collage wait until your partner finishes his.

TO MAKE THIS GAME MAXIMALLY EFFECTIVE, DO NOT READ AHEAD UNTIL YOU HAVE COMPLETED PART I. THE ELEMENT OF SURPRISE FOR ALL PARTICIPANTS GREATLY ADDS TO THE GAME.

Outline: Part II

When you have finished constructing your collage fantasies, *exchange your constructions.* You will now have your partner's collage, he will have yours. Look at your partner's collage and build a fantasy around it. If you wish, the fantasy activity around the collage need not have continuity or be a continuous story. (It does not have to be a progressive fantasy.) You may just wish to react to specific parts in your partner's collage and allow your fantasy stream to flow in relation to this part in a free association manner.

For example Jane had this reaction to her partner's collage:

"The eye that is on top of the cow's horn. The fantasy I have about this eye is that it fills the whole sky, and that I am in a field where all the flowers are lovely twinkling eyes. The cow with those horns is a bull. I am one of those lady matadors in Mexico about to enter the ring to fight a bull. . . ."

Look at your partner's collage and let your fantasy stream flow.

Outline: Part III (Optional)

After you have completed Part II take back your own collage and build a fantasy around it. Share this fantasy with your partner.

For Group Use

Team up in groups of two for this experience, and build a collage together. Suggest a time limit on the construction of the collage. Usually fifteen to twenty-five minutes is sufficient time for construction. Give participants a five-minute warning before the time is up. You can then follow through with Part II.

Another variation for a social group experience is to ask participants to volunteer sharing their fantasy in relation to their own collage construction while the group listens. A final variation is to obtain a large strip of butcher paper. Fasten this to the wall and have the group construct a collage together. Group members can then volunteer to present fantasies in relation to segments of the group collage.

THE FANTASY WALK

The main purpose of the fantasy walk is enjoyment. It can be played either by yourself or with a partner. The fantasy walk is best taken in a beautiful natural setting, although it may also be taken in a park or a similar environment. Choose a beautiful day for your walk.

Outline: Part I

As you walk along use various objects you encounter as "fantasy triggers." Let them trigger your fantasy and imagination and let your thoughts wander where they may.

The following are examples of fantasy triggers:

> *The shape of a tree*—seen from a distance—what does it suggest?
>
> *Cloud shapes*—lie on your back in a green and flowery field, look at the shapes of clouds, have fantasies and make up stories.
>
> *The bark of trees*—what shapes emerge as you look closely? Where do they lead you?
>
> *Flowers*—select one or several flowers that touch you with their beauty and let your fantasy go.
>
> *Sound of a brook*—can you hear rhythms, melodies, music, voices—what do they say?

Outline: Part II

As you walk, look for a spot you consider very beautiful. Sit down, relax and enjoy it—let your fantasies develop.

Outline: Part III

How about the microcosm experience? You've probably had it as a child. Find a green and beautiful spot and after you have enjoyed it a while, put your hand very close to the ground. Now close one eye and look at a small piece of ground very intently. Everything will appear greatly magnified and the blades of grass will look like a jungle. Let your imagination wander into this jungle. Let yourself go and follow the web it weaves.

Outline: Part IV

If you wish to use this technique, look at a cloud shape for example, and say to yourself, "Let my fantasy theme be a story about a maid and a giant." Then let the shape of the cloud determine the direction of the fantasy stream in conjunction with this theme or fit the cloud shape into the story.

Outline: Part V

Using free-flowing fantasy (without stating a fantasy theme in advance) let your imagination wander where the cloud shape leads it. Let different shapes in the cloud trigger your associations while you keep your eyes on the shape of the cloud. If your imagination wanders too far afield, you can bring it back to the cloud shape.

Outline: Part VI

If you take your fantasy walk with a partner, let stretches of this experience (or the total experience) be nonverbal. Not talking deepens the experience. Talk over your fantasy walk, if you wish, only after the experience.

Let this walk with fantasy unfold in you the joy of being.

**PARTNER ACTION
ALSO A GROUP GAME**

THE FEELIE BAG AND FEELIE WALK

It is well known that if a person allows himself the freedom to do so, certain stimuli with which he is presented will set off a chain of ideas and images. This is a form of free-association and can initiate an enjoyable form of fantasy play. At the same time this particular fantasy game can bring about a measure of sensory awakening as players experience new perspectives of sensing and feeling. This can be either an outdoor walking game or can be played at home.

Background

Some preliminary preparation is necessary for this game if it is to be played at home. To maintain the element of surprise, collect a wide variety of objects which have strong tactile qualities such as pieces of wood, twigs, stone, plastic, fur, cloth, velvet, clay or plasticine, feathers, leaves, flowers. Take three or four large grocery bags and place no more than six objects in each bag. Try for a "variety mix" in each "feelie bag" by including soft (fur, feathers) and hard articles (stones), smooth (plastic) and rough (bark or sandpaper). Avoid common household articles such as batteries or plastic spoons.

By preparing the grocery bags with the objects in them several days before the sensory association fantasy game is to be played, the person preparing for the game will forget the nature of some of the articles in the "feelie bag" and will be able to enjoy the game more.

For Group Use

The host should prepare the feelie bags in advance. The host can read relevant instructions and take the role of the partner to encourage fantasy experiencing. To add to the experience, place a cold piece of liver or cold cooked noodles in a plastic bag and add it to one of the feelie bags.

Feelie bags are passed from hand to hand and players volunteer fantasies if they wish as they touch and explore objects.

Outline: Part I—The Feelie Bag Game Played at Home

The partner hands the player a grocery bag containing sensory objects. He is told to close his eyes, put one hand in the "feelie bag," grasp and feel one single object. The instructions are:

> "Don't try to identify the nature of the object, keep your eyes closed, feel it and let ideas, thoughts and images come to your mind. If you want to, share some of these ideas, thoughts and images. If you want to, you can also have a fantasy or make up a story about some of the objects. Spend time with each object. As you are finished with the object take it out of the bag—but don't look at it. Don't open your eyes. Then go on to the next object."

(These instructions can be read aloud.)

Outline: Part II—The Feelie Walk

This is a walking game played outdoors, preferably in a park or in the country. The player is asked to close his eyes and to entrust himself to his partner. The partner then slowly leads the player from object to object, holding the player with one arm around the shoulder or waist, with the other hand holding his arm. Gently he guides the player's arm until his open hand touches the object he wants him to sense and explore. (If the player is right-handed, use of the left hand often intensifies the experience and vice versa.)

The player can now be led to a variety of objects with varying surfaces which offer differing sensory experience. Ask him not to talk and to flow with the experience.

Have him explore the smooth and rough bark of trees, stones, leaves, flowers, grass, earth, surface of a car, your own hair and clothes and so on.

Again, the objective of the game is *not* to identify objects, but with eyes closed to let images, ideas and associations flow freely.

During the walking game many players are so involved in the enjoyment of the sensory experience that they do not wish to verbalize. This is understandable and they should not be pressured to talk but to "let it happen."

Outline: Part III

Another dimension of this game is to ask the player to make up an ongoing fantasy (with eyes closed) incorporating the flow of ideas or images from each object or the nature of the object.

For example:

The player's hand touches a cold metal surface—"I am in Eskimo land and see an igloo. An Eskimo is emerging. . . ."

Hand touches stone:

"The Eskimo picks up a stone he sees and throws it at the bear's head, and manages to hit him in the eye."

DO NOT READ BEYOND THIS POINT. LET YOUR PARTNER'S ACTION BRING YOU THE SURPRISE OF NEW ADVENTURE.

Partner Action: Part I

A. Don't force or rush the player to share his fantasies. You may wish to remark:

"Take your time to let images and thoughts flow, let things happen. Talk about it when you feel like it."

B. If the player remains silent for four to five objects which he has touched and explored, gently urge: "Try to put some of the images and ideas you have into words. You select what you want to put into words. Use short unfinished sentences if you want to."

Partner Action: Part II

A. Try to introduce considerable variation into the sequence presented for your partner's sensory explorations—vary hard with soft surface, rough with smooth and so on.

B. If you are doing the feelie walk invite your partner to enjoy the experience of being led and being taken care of. Lead him gently and slowly. Warn him about curbs and obstacles. The objective is to make this a very positive trip into new sensory and imaginational horizons.

THE PRIMAL SENSORY EXPERIENCE

This group game offers an opportunity for a very loving and caring experience which six to twenty or more people can have together. The game is best played after the people present have been together for some time and have gotten to know each other. Some advance preparation is necessary: The host should obtain six to eight grapes (a variety having seeds) per person.

Background

The objective of the game is to create a caring, loving experience for all participants which fosters the flow of fantasies. The game should be played in a room which has carpeting, or, if there is no carpet, pillows can be furnished.

Outline: Part I

Announce the game in the following or similar words:

"We are going to play a game called the Primal Sensory Experience. We will divide into triads or groups of three. Each group will have at least one member of the opposite sex in it (i.e. two women, one man). The game requires that married or dating couples and lovers not be in the same triad.

"I am going to divide us into triads now. As soon as you have been divided, get to know the people in your triad. If you know them already, get to know them better. Ask questions you would not usually ask."

(The host should give triads five to ten minutes to get acquainted.)

Outline: Part II

After five to ten minutes, the host continues:

"I will repeat the instructions for this game twice so that everything is clear. This is a nonverbal experience which means no talking. The primal sensory experience involves three elements: rocking, stroking, feeding." (The host should print these three words in large letters on a piece of paper and show this to the group.)

"This can be a very positive loving and caring experience for everyone in your triad if you make it that way. *Use your fantasy during this experience and imagine you are either a parent or a child.*

"Now by *rocking* we mean sit on the floor, actually take the person in your lap, cradle his head on your shoulders and move the upper part of your body back and forth, rocking him (the host demonstrates). *Stroking* means a gentle stroking of the hair, face and body while he is being rocked (the host demonstrates). Have the person take his shoes off and don't forget to stroke his feet. Stroking is done mostly by the third member of the triad who is free to move around.

"For *feeding* we have six grapes per person. At least one grape should be fed peeled. Now, the grapes have seeds. The person being fed can either chew and swallow them or put them on his lips and one of the triad will remove them. Now, the person who is the center of attention is *rocked, stroked and fed as much as possible simultaneously.* He has all three experiences at the same time with his eyes closed. The basic ground rule is *if you think he has had enough, give him twice as long.* People rarely get enough of this experience.

"While you are being rocked, stroked and fed, let your fantasy go where it may. Enjoy and flow with it and with the experience."

(The host should repeat the instructions.)

Outline: Part III

"Now begin the experience by *nonverbally choosing one of your group* to be rocked, stroked and fed while his eyes are closed. Closing the eyes adds to the enjoyment of the experience."

The host can bring grapes to the triads and help in the

stroking. As triads are finished they should be encouraged to rest quietly so as not to disturb others who have not finished.

Outline: Part IV

The host now calls for a sharing of fantasies during the experience. "Would anyone care to share some of their fantasies during this experience?"

To close the experience, obtain feedback by asking the group the following question: "How do you feel now?"

FANTASY AND IMAGINATION —ON YOUR OWN

In this section you have an opportunity to enjoy your fantasy flow on your own.

This series of games will help you to expand and develop your creative ingenuity without anyone else's help. There are games designed to determine which circumstances or environments help your fantasy and imagination flow best. There are also games for analyzing and channeling your fantasy patterns. Finally, a method is offered for a transcendental or spiritual experience.

Joyous experiencing!

EXPANDING THE HORIZON OF YOUR FANTASY AND IMAGINATION

The production of fantasies seems to be determined by three major factors:

A. Internal emotional states, moods and attitudes

B. The direction, set, or goals toward which an individual is pointed

C. The external environment

Many persons have found that by understanding and controlling the latter two factors (especially the third), their fantasy experience and production was greatly enhanced.

Discovering what increases the productivity of your fantasy and imagination is not too difficult. You begin by examining your underlying attitude toward fantasies and the use of imagination. If you are deeply convinced that to have fantasies and use your imagination, *is a form of play through which we can grow,* then you are pointed in the direction where the use of fantasy can have maximum impact on the nature of your being and becoming.

If you believe the use of imagination is enjoyable creative play, a form of delight and enchantment which we need to give ourselves as much as possible, then your direction is such as to help you have many spontaneous, entrancing journeys into expanding the horizon of your fantasy and imagination—whence lies adventure.

Start by asking yourself the following key question:

Under what circumstances do my fantasy and imagination flow most freely?

Most people have difficulty answering this question because few persons are sufficiently self-aware to know under what circumstances their flow of fantasy and imagination is high.

Begin deliberately to try out different environments to determine which stimulate you, turn you on and encourage or facilitate the flow of your imagination and fantasy.

> Is the fantasy stream more enjoyable and free flowing
>> on the beach?
>> in the woods?
>> in a field?
>> in your home? (when?)
>> after a great meal with a loved person?
>> looking into the fire?
>> with someone? (who?)
>> alone?
>> walking in a park?
>> along a street?
>> on top of a hill?
>> riding in a car or on a horse?

Where, when and under what circumstances do you fantasize best? Can you discover what set of factors favors the emergence of that rippling stream which is your imagination?

As previously mentioned, one of the most important things in developing the flow of your fantasy and imagination is to verbalize your fantasy. Putting fantasies into words adds a new dimension to communication and imparts new freedom. Help your friends to accept your fantasy stream and in turn accept theirs. You can introduce the concept of fantasy casually by saying:

> "As I was walking along, I just had this fantasy; let me tell it to you."

How about discovering and deliberately using *fantasy triggers* (the shapes of clouds, bushes and trees, for example) to trigger the flow of fantasies?

By discovering what increases the productivity of our fantasy and imagination, we can become exultant explorers into the adventuresome interior of our limitless inner universe.

WE ARE AS BIG AND AS SMALL AS THE LIMITS OF OUR IMAGINATION. *As we expand the horizon of our imagination we come ever closer to unfolding that joyous self which is our creative core.*

FANTASY ON THE JOB

It is well known that everyone has fantasies and daydreams during the day. Sometimes the nature of our fantasies and daydreams while "on the job" differ markedly from those in other environments.

Fantasies are different from daydreams. Fantasies involve the (consciously) directed flow of imagination, images and ideas. Daydreams appear and disappear seemingly without volition—we do not consciously direct them: They come to us and we float with them willy-nilly. We usually forget daydreams almost immediately.

For example, some people have unhappy or sadistic fantasies about their superiors, or "escape" fantasies of "getting away from it all." The awareness of our own vocational fantasy life can result in increased self-understanding. Sometimes, such fantasies also indicate a route leading to action.

You can analyze the nature of your vocational fantasy life by watching yourself as you lapse into a daydream or fantasy while at work. For most people this added element of conscious awareness before or after the daydream or fantasy is not a disturbing factor. Others are so largely unconscious of their fantasies that they must first learn to pay conscious attention in order to recall the fantasy.

Fantasy retrieval can be greatly facilitated by this simple practice.

> Consciously set aside five to ten minutes daily and let your mind wander where it may.

> At the end of five minutes, recall the high points (and, if possible, details) of your fantasy.

With practice, greater ease in recall can usually be achieved in a relatively short time.

You may wish to keep notes over a period of days on the nature of your vocational fantasies.

To gain greater self-understanding and awareness, analyze your vocational fantasies in the light of the following:

> A. What is the nature of these fantasies?

> B. What patterns emerge? (Are there repetitions, i.e. same subject, theme or class?)

> C. What are the feelings which accompany the fantasies: neutral? slightly pleasant? pleasant? unpleasant?

> D. Should your increased understanding of your vocational fantasies lead to any change or action on your part?

The Productive Use of Vocational Fantasies

First, it is necessary to understand that it is healthy and normal to have fantasies, regardless of their content. Sadistic fantasies about a manager or administrator may be a form of working on a problem. Sometimes all that can be done is to enjoy the fantasy. More often than not, however, greater understanding of our fantasy life can lead to productive change and action on our part. If, for example, sadistic fantasies about a manager or administrator persist, a problem is clearly indicated. Once *aware* of a problem, alternative methods of coping with the difficulty can be explored.

Productive use of fantasies can also be achieved by directing the fantasy stream along certain lines. For example, a number of people have reported excellent results from application of the following method:

Consciously take a fantasy break. Set aside five to ten minutes daily when on the job. In that period, let your mind wander where you wish to channel it. Such a path may be:

What would improve this job?

How can I improve my functioning?

What creative or new ideas can I fantasize in relation to this (specific) project?

At first your fantasy stream may deviate from the channel in which you wish it to flow. Be gentle with yourself and bring it back again and again. At times "let yourself go" by following a fantasy away from the main channel, then redirect or refocus your fantasy stream back into the channel where you wish it to go. Again, practice will bring ever greater direction to your fantasy stream *and it will be an enjoyable experience.*

The main thing to remember while using this technique is

Do not be critical of your fantasy productivity.

Do not evaluate a fantasy product while you are in the midst of the fantasy stream. Take notes and assess the product later.

Let time elapse between fantasy productivity and assessment or evaluation.

Encourage any fantasy productivity. The more fantasies the merrier. Welcome the ever-changing stream—this is the stream of life! As you relax with the flow of quantity, quality will emerge. You can expect many encounters with the unexpected. Consistent use of your fantasies for vocational productivity is a means of giving yourself the experience of future growth and development.

THE "WOW"

This game puts us in touch with ourselves, our world and each other. It is particularly effective when driving alone to and from work, on long trips or vacations or the like. Objectives of the game are to increase awareness of one's environment and sensory inputs, to enhance self-understanding and self-awareness, to foster spontaneity, imagination and fantasy.

Outline: Part I

While driving along or while alone on a walk, open yourself to what you perceive is happening around you or rolling by the windows outside of your car. Even if it is "old scenery," things change and events happen.

> Open yourself to the color and shapes of a cloud in the sky or to a beautiful bush in bloom.

Search for beauty, for as you know, "beauty lies in the eyes of the beholder."

Open yourself to ugliness—*to anything that will stir and touch your emotions.*

Outline: Part II

As you are driving or walking along and anything touches you emotionally—WOW: immediately *associate out loud* anything that comes to your mind. (Some people have found it helpful to exclaim WOW in order to start the free association process.)

Free associate aloud and let words, ideas, thoughts and emotions flow wherever they want to go.

You will find very little movement and growth in yourself if you engage in internal dialogue, i.e. if you do not associate out loud, using your voice at any volume you wish. You must verbalize your associational flow. You may feel only slight tugs at first instead of the real WOW of emotional impact as you let beauty or ugliness in the environment touch you, and consequently your associational flow may be restricted. However, repeated and continued use of the method over a period of time will bring results. The longer you use the method the freer will be your associational flow and the more you will discover about yourself.

The various components of this experience in developing your potential appear to be as follows:

You open yourself to greater awareness of your environment through which you formerly passed mechanically. As you do this daily, you begin to see beauty and events you never saw before. You begin to see beauty (and ugliness) *in other situations and environments.* Ultimately, this can lead to increased awareness of beauty and disharmony in all spheres of life, including discovering more beauty in the personality of people. You become more sensitive to all that is around you.

As you let an event or perception touch you:

> "Ah, there is a beautiful bush in full bloom—its yellow golden color sparkles in the sunlight— WOW!"

You are becoming more aware of your feelings and emotions. You let your emotions unfold and irradiate your being—you flow with them and through them. You are engaged in the process of vitalizing and regenerating affective components of yourself. You begin to be more aware of the vital role of emotions in the process of self-realization and growth.

As you free associate out loud, let the words come:

> "The beautiful yellow bush—golden, the sun, bathing in the sun, being at one with warmth and love. . . ."

You are engaged in a spontaneous act of self-revelation.

You are partaking of spontaneity.

As you listen to your words with your "third ear" you deepen your self-understanding

> "Aha! I need the sun, the warmth, the love!"

and add to your self-awareness.

As you free associate and let your words roll out loud and unimpeded, you are fostering the development of imagination and fantasy. If you want to, you can push this process even further and build a fantasy around that yellow blooming bush, letting it lead you where it wants to go.

It is of the essence of the WOW method that it helps us be more profoundly in touch with our world, with ourselves and with each other. It is through this "in-touchness" that we can become our possibilities.

THE OCEANIC EXPERIENCE

Anyone who wishes can have the experience of an oceanic fantasy. Oceanic fantasies are:

Feeling oneness with the earth or the ocean
Feeling oneness with God or the universe
Feeling oneness with all being
Feeling in tune with all creation
Feeling limitless and boundless.

A full and successful oceanic fantasy experience has some of all of the following components:
A feeling of deep peace

of being part of a greater whole
of exaltation
of ecstasy
of great gladness and joy, tranquility, deep contentment and fulfillment.

Sometimes it is helpful to read accounts of mystical and peak experiences. Perhaps most important is an openness to the experience.

Outline: Part I

Achieving a satisfactory oceanic fantasy experience may require awareness of the circumstances and environment which can bring forth a feeling of oneness and exaltation in you.

Is it being on the beach near the ocean?

On top of a mountain?

In a pine forest with the wind blowing and no other sound?

On top of a high building in the city?

Explore which is the most favorable environment for you—which brings you a feeling of peace and at-oneness.

Outline: Part II

You may now wish to proceed to the place you have selected. Once you arrive,

> recall or think about the most peaceful and serene moments in your life—the times you were most at peace with yourself. (These help you get into the right mood.)

You are now ready to have your oceanic fantasy. Closing your eyes and letting it happen are helpful. (Sit or stand quietly.)

Several attempts may be necessary before you have a successful oceanic fantasy experience. The practice attempts will point you in the right direction and help you determine what, for you, are the best physical and emotional conditions for this experience.

The next time you are ready and the circumstances are right, what you have read (and experienced) up to now has set the stage. *It is the purpose of the oceanic fantasy experience to help you reach that boundlessness which is you.*

GROUP FANTASY GAMES

A series of exciting and easy-to-play group experiences and social games is offered at the beginning of this section. The first three games are of an introductory nature, easy to play and enjoyable for groups with no previous experience in fantasy gaming.

Remember with slight changes, most group games can also be played by two people. Many of the duo-games and sensory fantasy games can also be used for group or social games. These have been marked ALSO A GROUP GAME in the upper right-hand corner of the page.

FANTASY SENTENCES

This action game can give spontaneous fun and excitement to any party or other group gathering. It can be either written or played orally. If your group is too large (twelve or more players), it may be best to play a written game and hand out pencils and papers. Even if your group decides to play it orally, some people like to write things down and then read what they have written.

Outline: Part I

Begin by asking for a volunteer to read the fantasy sentences.

Next, read out the following instructions:

"All you do is close your eyes, listen carefully and let your fantasy and imagination go.

Complete the sentence you hear in any way that comes to your mind.

Let your imagination flow freely.

Complete the fantasy sentences either in your mind or by writing it down.

You will then have an opportunity to share your fantasy with everyone else."

Outline: Part II

If you decide to play a written game, everyone completes the sentence on paper and then takes turns reading aloud or repeating it from memory. Announce:

"If you don't want to take your turn for one reason or another, just say, 'I pass.' "

Here are some sample fantasy sentences to begin the game. (Make up your own, too!)

Fantasy Sentences

1. "You are lying on your back in the shade beside a beautiful mountain stream. The sun is out . . . the sky is blue . . . there is a gentle wind, and you smell the grass and flowers around you. As you are lying there . . . ."

2. "A cross-country bus makes a rest stop in a small desert town out in the far West. The driver calls out that it is time to leave when he discovers . . . ."

3. "A girl dressed in blue jeans and a red and white checkered shirt is climbing up a trail in the mountains. It's a fairly steep trail and there are bushes hiding the next turn. She turns the corner and finds . . . ."

4. "You are standing under a canopy waiting for the summer shower to stop so you can move on, when the sound of the rain brings to mind . . . ."

5. "You hear this odd noise and out of the sky comes a very strange looking vehicle. It lands very softly, a little distance away from you, something like a door opens, and . . . ."

Variations

If you have a small group and want to use the fantasy sentences game as an adventure in imagination, those who wish to can

> tell a story of what happens to the central character of each fantasy sentence after the sentence is completed.

If you are by yourself you can write out the completion of the sentences on a piece of paper.

YOUR DREAM COME TRUE

This is a very enjoyable fantasy game for your next informal get-together. Make paper and pencil available to players who wish to use them.

Simply read the following instructions (suggest that people close their eyes as this may help them to fantasize better):

> "You have just had a tremendous stroke of luck. Good fortune has smiled on you and you have won a very large sum of money. At the same time, all of your obligations and responsibilities are taken care of. People have suddenly volunteered to help you out because they recognize that this good fortune comes but once in a lifetime. You can leave your job if you want to and return to it at some future time. Everything is possible to you now. You can do anything you want."

Now have the fantasy of your dream come true. It is simply this:

> What would you do if you inherited a very large sum of money and all of your obligations and responsibilities were taken care of?
> Where would you go?
> What is your dream about yourself and the glorious future ahead of you?

Follow your fantasy. Remember, your dream has come true, and you can do anything you want to.

If you want to, you can outline your fantasy on a piece of paper using key words and key sentences.

Now call for volunteers to tell about their dream come true. Announce that if they wish, they can close their eyes while sharing their fantasy with the group.

THE DONOVAN FANTASY

Although this fantasy can be fun when you are alone, it is even more enjoyable in a group.

Background

This game is based on the Donovan song, "A Legend of a Girl Child, Linda," found in the album *Sunshine Superman*, EPIC, L.N. 24217. This is one of the early Donovan songs—very rich in imagery. A good hi-fi or stereo sound system is needed. Read the following aloud:

Outline: Part I

"In preparation for the experience, close your eyes for about three minutes. Let fantasies about children playing on the beach and fantasies of medieval times come in; try to have these fantasies in color." (PAUSE)

Outline: Part II

Start "A Legend of a Girl Child, Linda."

"Now please close your eyes if you wish. Let yourself go with the images of the song. Create the scenes and images of Donovan's song in your mind—in color if you want. Let the images flow. Follow your fantasy stream!"

Outline: Part III

Now ask for volunteers to share images, fantasies and experiences which participants had during the playing of the song.

THE HAPPIEST FANTASY OF YOUR CHILDHOOD

Another chance for an enjoyable experience can be found in this game which "takes you back to your childhood." (This is also a duo-game which can be played with a partner.)

Suggestions

Read the following to the group:

What was the happiest fantasy of your childhood? Were you the central figure in a fairy tale or story of adventure?

Were you a hero in sports or a central figure in the movies?

Were you a prince or princess?

A cowboy?

A locomotive engineer?

Was your happiest fantasy one of being a person or an animal?

Pause briefly. Then continue reading:

You may now wish to close your eyes as this often facilitates fantasizing.

Think back to the times when you were small, when you were a child back home. Recall your happiest fantasy as a child. If you cannot remember, imagine what your happiest fantasy in childhood might have been. Make one up.

THE FANTASY DICE GAME

This is a fast-moving game which is particularly effective if played in a group but may also be played by two persons. If the game is used in a group it can be an effective ice-breaker and can function as an introduction to social fantasy games.

Background

If this game is to be used in a group, some advance preparation is necessary. A single die should be secured.

(Slips of paper numbered one to six drawn from a brown paper bag may be used if dice are not handy.) Write the following with a marking pen in big block letters on a large sheet of paper (or two standard sheets of paper can be pasted together):

Die Point List

1. A fantasy of success
2. A fantasy of escape
3. A fantasy of beauty
4. A fantasy of fear
5. A fantasy of joy
6. A fantasy of love (can be sexual)

Outline: Part I

Players sit facing each other or in a circle. If in a group, spin a bottle to determine whose turn it is to throw the die. The die point list should be conspicuously posted so that everyone can see it. Each person throws his own die.

If the die comes up with the "5," for example, the person who has thrown the die (or drawn the number from the bag) should now share a fantasy of joy. If it is agreeable and would be fun for the group, other members could add to the fantasy after the person has finished his fantasy of joy.

Should a much deeper type of individual or group experience be desired, the following *first* ground rule should be agreed to and announced: "EACH FANTASY SHOULD INVOLVE THE PERSON GIVING THE FANTASY AS THE CENTRAL FIGURE—USE THE PRONOUN 'I.'" By this device third-person fantasies are successfully eliminated.

If this game is to be used as an ice-breaker and introduction to fantasy encounter group games, it is *well to wait before announcing* this ground rule until about half the people have had their turn.

Another dimension of intimacy can be added to the game by the following *second* ground rule: "LET THE PEOPLE IN YOUR FANTASY BE PEOPLE FROM THIS GROUP—THIS APPLIES TO ALL NUMBERS OF THE DIE EXCEPT NUMBER SIX."

The latter half of this ground rule may be omitted but it should be clearly understood that this omission may raise the anxiety level in the group and cause considerable tension. It is not recommended that the *second* ground rule be used initially if the game is employed as an ice-breaker at the beginning of a party or social occasion.

THE FANTASY ADVENTURE

The adventure and fantasy game is designed to help renew an appetite for the zest of life we call adventuring.

Suggestions

Read the following introduction to those present:

"Almost everyone loves adventures and adventuring—their own or someone else's. For some of us, the sense of adventuring lends a quality of spice and vitality to life that otherwise seems dull.

"We can adventure while involved in even the most routine and dull circumstances *if we want to* and if we are willing to use our imagination. Life is and can be an adventure if we would only make it that way. The quality of adventuring which we experience largely depends on two factors:

1. The measure of self-risk

2. Our ability to use imagination and fantasy to become aware of, to form and even to experience the adventure. (More often than we would care to admit, we *are* engaged in an adventure, but we need to become aware of this fact through the spontaneous illumination which springs from our use of imagination.)"

Now ask everyone to take five minutes of silent time to think of an adventure.

"Ask yourself this question:

What was the greatest adventure I have had during my life?

"Close your eyes and relive it, remembering as many details as you can.

"If you have not had an adventure, or don't wish to share any particular adventure

you can make up an adventure that you would like to have.

"You may also wish to use a real adventure you have had and embroider it, add to it, change it or elaborate on it. For example,

how you would have *liked* a certain incident to end.

"You could also add elements of make-believe to an adventure you have had and make it even greater than it was."

At this point give everyone five minutes of silent time. Say that you will announce when time is up. Suggest that they close their eyes as this often improves fantasizing.

When time is up, state there is only one ground rule:

"No one, should ask anyone whether the adventure which is shared is real, partly make-believe or fantasy, either privately or in the group."

Now ask for volunteers to share their fantasy.

After everyone who wants to has had his turn, or after there has been some ongoing adventure sharing, you may wish to bring the experience to a close by discussing one or more of the following questions:

1. Is life as an adventure a desirable concept?

2. How can we make life more of an adventure?

.

THE BRAINSTORMING FANTASY

This is a fast-moving game which encourages the emergence of fantasies. It is a great experience to tape record and play back to the group.

Suggestions

Everyone sits in a circle.

As host you can slowly read the following instructions:

"One of us volunteers to begin. He starts by saying *three consecutive sentences* which pop into his mind. After the first person has said his three sentences, he flips a coin. If the toss comes up heads, the person sitting to the right of him is next and so on around the circle. If tails, the person to the left of him is next and the turns go around to the left. *Only three sentences are added by each person.* These may or may not be related to the previous person's sentences.

"The focus is on letting your fantasies go—go—go! If they are triggered by what the other person said, great! If not, equally great! For example, one person said:

> 'As far as my eyes could see, there was a rosy glow
> and the gentle but pervasive smell of happiness. As
> the flowers opened themselves and poured forth
> their gladness, ecstasy was in the air. Then came
> the festive stirring of something about to happen.'

"If you are temporarily blocked, let your turn go by. Merely point to the person next to you. Do not say a word to break the spell of the developing and rippling fantasy wave. The turn will go around one more time to give those who were blocked or who wanted to fantasize silently a chance to verbalize if they wish.

"(Remember you can participate silently if you want to, with the knowledge that expressing the fantasy in words may be a freeing experience for you.)

"There are only two major ground rules for this experience:

1. Only three sentences per person each turn.

2. No psychologizing, analyzing or interpreting other people's fantasies. Being the analyst or 'shrink' in this context of play is a type of *one-upmanship* which should be avoided.

"Some people prefer to close their eyes while listening to other people's three-sentence fantasies."

Have fun!

A PERSON-CENTERED FANTASY EXPERIENCE

Usually played as a paper and pencil game, this fantasy adventure works best in a group. If you are by yourself, or with a partner, you can play it by choosing someone you know and whom you are likely to meet face to face in a day or two.

Suggestions

Slowly read the following to the group:

"Look at the people in the group. Choose anyone in the room. Let it be someone you know fairly well. *Don't let them know that you have chosen them.*

"Now close your eyes and let the image of this person appear on your mental horizon.

Think about him. Think about everything this person has done throughout his or her life. Now you are ready to have a fantasy about this person."

Hand out paper and pencil, then read:

"Write down what this person could accomplish if he had all the money and power to develop his talents the way he wanted. What could he accomplish with all that money and power? You may want to write at the top of your sheet 'Accomplishments.'

"Next, on the lower half of your sheet write down what discoveries and adventures this person might make or have. You may want to write the key words "Discoveries and Adventures" on the lower half of your sheet of paper. You may also want to use key words and key sentences on your paper instead of writing out everything in longhand."

Tell the group they have about ten minutes to do the person-centered fantasy.

Now call for volunteers to share their fantasy. Mention that

"If you want to you can announce the name of the person you have chosen for your fantasy and then share the fantasy. If there isn't enough time to get around to everyone, you can, if you wish, share your fantasy privately after the game with the person you have selected."

THE OPEN-ENDED GROUP FANTASY

Take a trip anywhere with this fantasy. This is a fast-moving, exciting game.

Suggestions

The group members select the setting where the fantasy takes place, and where they will take part in an adventure.

This could be a jungle with a tribe of natives nearby, a cabin by the seashore, a forest inhabited by elves, magicians and demons, or a tropical island, etc.

Outline: Part I

Decide on the setting and describe the environment of the setting, i.e. what type of jungle, how does the cabin look, how it is finished. This is done on a voluntary basis, with *everyone spontaneously* sharing their ideas about environmental details.

Outline: Part II

Take turns creating and sharing in the developing adventure. For example, a group having a jungle fantasy began their fantasy:

> Bob—"Jim was walking down the jungle path carrying some flowers and fruit when suddenly he met Jane" (a group member).

> Lilly—"Jane saw him and said, 'How about giving me some fruit?' He shook his head but before he could say anything the drums of the natives started in the distance. They heard running steps and here came Mary, Tim and Bob" (group members).

There should be no orderly taking of turns. Each person calls out spontaneously, adding to the fantasy whenever he wishes.

ACTION FANTASY

Here is an opportunity to act out a favorite fantasy with the help of friends. Since our culture seems to inculcate a great deal of shyness, withholding and fear of risk-taking in its members, this method works best in a group where these elements are minimally present. The more open, authentic, creative, risk-taking, and giving the group, the greater the possibility that the action fantasy will become a means of personal growth for all involved.

Suggestions

Someone volunteers to be the fantasy director. It is the task of the fantasy director to *direct and live out his own fantasy with the group's help.*

A. The fantasy director selects a fantasy in which he is the central figure, and which he would like to see translated into action. He shares this fantasy in detail with the group.

B. He begins by describing, in detail, the environment of the fantasy. Simple props can be used and the group can help fill in details of the setting by adding their suggestions.

C. Since more than one character (or animal) is usually involved in the action fantasy, *each character should be described in detail by the fantasy director.* Particular attention should be given to the

type of person each character is, how he behaves,
what his mood and feelings are and so on. The
fantasy director can ask for a volunteer to act out
each character as he finishes describing him. (The
group may wish to add their own suggestions to
this description, but these suggestions should be in
line with the fantasy director's characterization.)

If possible, the total group should become involved in the
action fantasy. Members can become animals, crowds, trees
or other objects at the bidding of the director.

D. The fantasy is now set in motion by the director who starts the action. Use your imagination
and spontaneity as much as possible in carrying out
the fantasy. Try to make the fantasy come true in
this moment of time. Everyone should feel their
way into the characters, animals, or things they
have been asked to represent. Remember, your
primary goal is to help the director live out his
fantasy.

The following are some examples of action fantasies
chosen by players:

A. "I am a king and you are my court."

B. "I am a saint in a forest and speak to the
animals" (group became trees, flowers and animals).

C. "God (that's me), the devil, angels, and souls to
be judged."

D. "I've always wanted to be the conductor of a
symphony orchestra" (group became musicians
while his favorite record was played).

E. "I choose being a widely acclaimed artist"
(group admired his works and gave applause).

ADDITIONAL LIST OF GROUP FANTASY ENCOUNTER GAMES

Some of the duo and sensory fantasy games can easily be adapted to group use. The following list of games can be played in small or large groups.

APPENDIX A.

List of Growth Centers

The list of centers presented here is by no means complete, and inclusion here does not necessarily imply an endorsement. The listings is included to inform the reader about organizations presently known for their work in this highly significant new field.

NEW ENGLAND

Associates for Human Resources
387 Sudbury Road
Concord, Mass. 01742

Boston Tea Party
55 Berkeley Street
Boston, Mass. 02116

Cumbres
Box C
Dublin, N.H. 03444

Foundation for Gifted and
   Creative Children
395 Diamond Hill Road
Warwick, R.I. 02866

Human Relations Center
Boston University
270 Bay State Road
Boston, Mass. 02215

Human Resources Development
Hidden Springs
South Acworth, N.H. 03607

Institute for Experimental
   Education
Box 446
Lexington, Mass. 02173

Lifwyn Foundation
52 South Morningside Drive
Westport, Conn. 06880

New England Center for Personal
   and Organizational Development
Box 575
Amherst, Mass. 01002

Number Nine
266 State Street
New Haven, Conn. 06511

Sky Farm Institute
Maple Corner
Calais, Vt. 05648

MIDDLE ATLANTIC

Anthos
24 East 22nd Street
New York, N.Y. 10010

Encounters: Workshops in Personal and Professional Growth
5225 Connecticut Avenue, NW
Suite 209
Washington, D.C. 20015

Groups for Meaningful
Communication
645 West End Avenue
New York, N.Y. 10025

G.R.O.W.
312 West 82nd Street
New York, N.Y. 10024

Human Dimensions Institute
4380 Main Street
Buffalo, N.Y. 14226

Human Resources Institute
Box 3296
Baltimore, Md. 21228

Humanist Society of Greater
New York
2109 Broadway at 73rd Street
New York, N.Y. 10023

Athena Center for Creative
Living
2308 Smith Avenue
Aliquippa, Pa. 15001

Awosting Retreat
315 West 57th Street
New York, N.Y. 10019

Bucks County Seminar House
Erwinna, Pa. 18920

Center for Human Development
217 North Craig Street
Pittsburgh, Pa. 15213

Center for the Whole Person
1633 Race Street
Philadelphia, Pa. 19103

Community Consultation Services
285 Central Park West
New York, N.Y. 10024

Dialogue House Associates
45 West 10th Street
New York, N.Y. 10011

Instad—Institute for Training
and Development
625 Stanwix Street, Suite 2306
Pittsburgh, Pa. 15222

Institute for Living
300 South 19th Street
Philadelphia, Pa. 19103

Institute for Rational Living
45 East 65th Street
New York, N.Y. 10021

Institute for Research into
Personal Freedom
327 Sixth Avenue
New York, N.Y. 10014

Institute of Applied
Psychotherapy
251 West 92nd Street
New York, N.Y. 10025

Interface, Inc.
Park Plaza No. 534
1629 Columbia Road, NW
Washington, D.C. 20015

Ithaca Seed Company
Box 651
Ithaca, New York 14850

Kirkridge
Bangor, Pa. 18013

Laboratory for Applied
Behavioral Science
Newark State College
Union, N.J. 07083

Mid-Atlantic Institute of
Christian Education
Suite 325
1500 Massachusetts Ave., NW
Washington, D.C. 20005

New York Institute for the
Achievement of Human
Potential
36 East 36th Street
New York, N.Y. 10016

N.T.L. Institute for Applied
  Behavioral Science
1201 Sixteenth Street, N.W.
Washington, D.C. 20036

Orizon Institute
2710   36th Street, NW
Washington, D.C. 20007

Pendle Hill
Wallingford, Pa. 19086

Personal Growth Laboratories
112 Hunter Lane
North Wales, Pa. 19454

Plainfield Consultation Center
831 Madison Avenue
Plainfield, N.J. 07060

Princeton Associates for
  Human Resources
341 Nassau Street
Princeton, N.J. 08540

Quest
3000 Connecticut Avenue, NW
Washington, D.C. 20008

Relationship Development Center
P.O. Box 23, Gedney Station
White Plains, N.Y. 10605

Sensitivity Training for
  Educational Personnel
Herbert H. Lehman College
Bedford Park Boulevard West
Bronx, N.Y. 10468

Sentio
247 West 72nd Street
New York, N.Y. 10023

Spruce Institute
1828 Spruce Street
Philadelphia, Pa. 19103

Tao House
522 Eastbrook Road
Ridgewood, N.J. 07450

Tarrytown House
Box 222
Tarrytown, N.Y. 10592

Training for Living Institute
80 Fifth Avenue
New York, N.Y. 10011

Wainwright House
Milton Point
Rye, N.Y. 10580

W.I.L.L. (Workshop Institute for
  Living-Learning)
333 Central Park West
New York, N.Y. 10025

SOUTH

Adanta
3379 Peachtree Road, NE
Suite 250
Atlanta, Ga. 30326

Atlanta Workshop for
  Living-Learning
3167 Rilman Road, NW
Atlanta, Ga. 30327

The Center
Box 157
Syria, Va. 22743

The Center of Man
Micanopy, Fla. 32667

Espiritu
1214 Miramar
Houston, Tex. 77006

The Family Relations Institute
3509 Farm Hill Drive
Annandale, Va. 22044

The Han Institute
c/o Denis O'Donovan
Executive Suite N
Weir Plaza Building
855 South Federal Highway
Boca Raton, Fla. 33432

Hara, Inc.
7322 Blairview
Dallas, Tex. 75230

Heliotrope
Box 9041
Fort Lauderdale, Fla. 33312

Keystone Experience
West Georgia College
Psychology Department
Carrollton, Ga. 30117

The Laos House: Southwest
  Center for Human Potential
700 West 19th
Austin, Tex. 78701.

Maitreyan Foundation
220 SW 2nd Street
Boca Raton, Fla. 33432

Omega Institute
Box 263
Merrifield, Va. 22116

The Piedmont Program
Box 6129
Winston-Salem, N.C. 27109

S.I.P.O.D.
2606 East Grove
Houston, Tex. 77027

Southwest Motivation Center, Inc.
Cambridge Tower
1801 Lavaca
Austin, Tex. 78701

MIDDLE WEST

Alverna Retreat House
8140 Spring Mill Road
Indianapolis, Ind. 46260

Amare: The Institute of
  Human Relatedness
Box 108
Bowling Green, Ohio 43402

Antioch Group for Human
  Relations
Antioch College
Yellow Springs, Ohio 45387

Cambridge House
1900 North Cambridge Avenue
Milwaukee, Wis. 53202

Center for Creative Interchange
602 Center Street
Des Moines, Ia. 50309

Communication Center No. 1
1001 Union Boulevard
St. Louis, Mo. 63113

Creative Risk-Taking Laboratories:
  Training Consultants
  International
Suite 132, 7710 Computer Avenue
Minneapolis, Minn. 55435

Domus
2722 Park Avenue
Minneapolis, Minn. 55407

Forest Growth Center
555 Wilson Lane
Des Plaines, Ill. 60016

Gestalt Institute of Cleveland
12921 Euclid Avenue
Cleveland, Ohio 44112

Greenerfields Unlimited
1740 Waukegan Road
Glenview, Ill. 60025

Human Potential
Unity Village, Mo. 64063

Human Resources Developers
520 North Michigan
Chicago, Ill. 60611

Inscape
2845 Comfort
Birmingham, Mich. 48010

Kopavi
Box 16
Wayzata, Minn. 55391

Midwest Personal Growth Center
200 South Hanley Road
Clayton, Mo. 63105

Oasis: Midwest Center for
  Human Potential
20 East Harrison
Chicago, Ill. 60605

Omega Center
Unity Village, Mo. 64063

Ontos, Inc.
40 South Clay
Hindsdale, Ill. 60521

Outreach
University of Michigan
Psychology Department
Ann Arbor, Mich. 48104

People
4340 Campbell
Kansas City, Mo. 64110

Seminars for Group Studies
Center for Continuing Education
University of Chicago
1307 East 60th Street
Chicago, Ill. 60637

Shadybrook House
Rural Route 1
Mentor, Ohio 44060

University Associates
Box 24402
Indianapolis, Ind. 46224

University Associates
Box 615
Iowa City, Ia. 52240

Uomes
110 Anderson Hall
University of Minnesota
Minneapolis, Minn. 55455

NORTHWEST

Northwest Family Therapy
  Institute
Box 94278
Tacoma, Wash. 98494

Seminars in Group Process
8475 SW Bohmann Parkway
Portland, Ore. 97223

Senoi Institute, Inc.
Route 2, Box 259
Eugene, Ore. 97401

Star Weather Ranch Institute
Box 923
Hailey, Ida. 83333

MOUNTAIN

Arizona Training Laboratories for
  Applied Behavioral Science
Box 26660
Tempe, Ariz. 85281

Evergreen Institute
3831 West Wagon Trail Drive
Littleton, Col. 80120

Institute of General Semantics
University of Denver
Denver, Col. 80210

Rocky Mountain Behavioral
  Institute
12086 West Green Mountain Dr.
Denver, Col. 80228

Vida
Ventures in Developing Awareness
1934 East Charleston
Las Vegas, Nev. 89104

Yogi Academy Foundation
3209 Burton Avenue, SE
Albuquerque, N.M. 87107

CALIFORNIA

Analysis Institute
1394 Westwood Boulevard
Los Angeles, Calif. 90024

Berkeley Center for Human
  Interaction
1820 Scenic
Berkeley, Calif. 94709

Berkeley Institute for Training in
  Group Therapy and Psychodrama
1868 San Juan Avenue
Berkeley, Calif. 94707

Berkeley Movers
4919 Clarke Street
Oakland, Calif. 94609

Bindrim, Paul & Associates
2000 Cantata Drive
Los Angeles, Calif. 90028

Blue Mountain Center of
    Meditation
1960 San Antonio
Berkeley, Calif. 94707

Bridge Mountain Foundation
2011 Alba Road
Ben Lomond, Calif. 95005

Casaelya
2266 Union Street
San Francisco, Calif. 94123

The Center
Box 3014
•Stanford, Calif. 94305

The Center for Creativity
    and Growth
599 College Avenue
Palo Alto, Calif. 94306

Center for Human Communication
120 Oak Meadow Drive
Los Gatos, Calif. 95030

Center for Interpersonal
    Development
3127 Eastern Avenue
Sacramento, Calif. 95821

Center for Studies of the Person
1125 Torrey Pines Road
La Jolla, Calif. 92037

Counseling Associates
30 South El Camino Real
San Mateo, Calif. 94401

Counseling Associates
6275 Shadygrove Court
San Jose, Calif. 95129

Dialogue House Associates
Box 877
San Jacinto, Calif. 92383.

Edmucko
P.O. Box 216
Ben Lomond, Calif. 95005

Elysium Institute
5436 Fernwood Avenue
Los Angeles, Calif. 90027

Emotional Studies Institute
775 Camino del Sur C-2
Goleta, Calif. 93017

Esalen Institute
Big Sur, Calif. 93920

Esalen Institute
1776 Union Street
San Francisco, Calif. 94123

Esalen Institute
Stanford University
Stanford, Calif. 94305

Eureka Center for Communicatio
    and Encounter
4300 Crest View Drive
Eureka, Calif. 95501

Explorations Institute
Box 1254
Berkeley, Calif. 94701

Foundation for Human
    Achievement
291 Geary Street
San Francisco, Calif. 94102

Gestalt Therapy Institute of
    Los Angeles
337 South Beverly Drive
Suite 206
Beverly Hills, Calif. 90212

Gestalt Therapy Institute of
    San Diego
7255 Girard Avenue, Suite 27
La Jolla, Calif. 92037

Gestalt Therapy Institute of
    Southern California
1029 Second Street
Santa Monica, Calif. 90403

Guild for Psychological Studies
2230 Divisadero Street
San Francisco, Calif. 94115

High Point Foundation
1001 East Rosecrans Avenue
Compton, Calif. 90221

Human Dynamics Workshop
Box 342
Boulder Creek, Calif. 95006

Human Potential Institute
2550 Via Tejon
Palos Verdes Estates, Calif. 90274

Human Resources Institute
1745 South Imperial Avenue
El Centro, Calif. 92243

Human Resources Institute
7946 Ivanhoe Avenue
La Jolla, Calif. 92037

Humanist Institute
1430 Masonic Street
San Francisco, Calif. 94117

Institute for Creative and Artistic
    Development
5935 Manchester Drive
Oakland, Calif. 94618

Institute for Group and Family
    Studies
347 Alma
Palo Alto, Calif. 94301

Institute for Growth
3627 Sacramento Street
San Francisco, Calif. 94118

Institute for Integrative
    Psychology
School of Social Sciences
University of California
Irvine, Calif. 92664

Institute for Multiple
    Psychotherapy
3701 Sacramento Street
San Francisco, Calif. 94118

Institute of Ability
P.O. Box 798
Lucerne Valley, Calif. 92356

Institute of Behavioral Dynamics
9000 Sunset Boulevard
Los Angeles, Calif. 90069

Institute of Human Abilities
80 Hamilton Place
Oakland, Calif. 94612

International Cooperation Council
17819 Roscoe Boulevard
Northridge, Calif. 93124

Kairos
The Ranch
Box 350
Rancho Santa Fe, Calif. 92067

Kairos
Town House
624 Upas Street
San Diego, Calif. 92103

Kemery Institute
304 Parkway
Chula Vista, Calif. 92010

Lafayette Center for Counseling
    and Education
Brook Dewing Medical Building
914 Dewing Street
Lafayette, Calif. 94549

National Center for the Exploration
    of Human Potential
8080 El Paseo Grande
La Jolla, Calif. 92037

New Consciousness Program
Old Student Union, Room 142
University of California
Santa Barbara, Calif. 93101

Pacific Training Associates
3516 Sacramento Street
San Francisco, Calif. 94118

Palo Alto Venture
P.O. Box 11802
Palo Alto, Calif. 94306

Personal Exploration Groups
2400 Bancroft Way
Stiles Hall
Berkeley, Calif. 94704

San Francisco Gestalt Therapy
   Institute
1719 Union Street
San Francisco, Calif. 94123

San Francisco Venture
584 Page Street
San Francisco, Calif. 94117

Schiffman, Muriel, Communication
   and Self Therapy Workshops
340 Santa Monica Avenue
Menlo Park, Calif. 94025

S.E.L.F. Institute
40 Hawthorne Avenue
Los Altos, Calif. 94022

Self-Other Systems Institute
Maple Street
Redwood City, Calif. 94063

Society for Comparative
   Philosophy, Inc.
Box 857
Sausalito, Calif. 94965

Sweet's Mill
Auberry, Calif. 93602

Tahoe Institute
Box DD
South Lake Tahoe, Calif. 95705

Thomas Jefferson Research Cente
1143 North Lake Avenue
Pasadena, Calif. 91104

Topanga Center for Human
   Development
2247 Topanga Canyon Road
Topanga, Calif. 90290

Viewpoints Institute
833 North Kings Road
Los Angeles, Calif. 90069

Well-Springs
2003 Alba Road
Ben Lomond, Calif. 95005

Western Center Consultants
9400 Culver Boulevard
Suite 206
Culver City, Calif. 90230

HAWAII

Human Explorations Program
P.O. Box 1145
Kanehoe, Hawaii 96744

CANADA

Claremont Experiment
P.O. Box 123
Weston, Ont.

Cold Mountain Institute
P.O. Box 2884
Vancouver, B.C.

Cold Mountain Institute
P.O. Box 4362
Edmonton 60, Alba.

Dynacom
2955 Fendall
Montreal 250, Que.

The Gestalt Training Institute
   of Canada
Lake Cowichan, Box 39
Vancouver, B.C.

Human Development Association
P.O. Box 811, Station B
Montreal, Que.

Shalal
750 West Broadway
Vancouver, B.C.

Strathmere
North Gower, Ont.

Synergia
P.O. Box 1685, Station B
Montreal 2, Que.

Toronto Growth Centre
Box 11
Downsview, Ont.

FOREIGN

Apartado Postal 85
San Miguel de Allende
Guanajuato, Mexico

Esalen-in-Chile
c/o Claudio Naranjo
1413 Allston Way
Berkeley, Calif. 94702

John C. Lilly
c/o Oscar Ichazo
Casilla 614
Arika, Chile

Tarango-Centro de Desarrollo
   Humano
Norte 59 No. 896
Industrial Vallejo
Mexico 16, D.F.

Yoloti
Sierra Vertientes 365
Mexico D.F. 10, Mexico

Australian Institute of Human
   Relations
12 Webb Street
Altona, Australia

Human Interaction Seminars
Box 4984
G.P.O. Sydney 2001 NSW
Australia

Center House
10-A Airlie Gardens
Kensington, London W8, England

Centre for Applied Social Research
The Tavistock Institute
Belzise Lane
London NW 3, England

M. Ferdinand Cuvelier
179 Passtraat
Geel, Belgium

Diipf
Box 900280, Schloss Straase 29
6 Frankfurt 90, Germany

Quaesitor
Vernon Road
Sutton, Surrey, England

APPENDIX B.

The Fantasy Acceleration Technique

If it is agreeable to both partners playing a particular game, the fantasy acceleration technique can be used. This technique can bring increased excitement and spontaneity. Use of this method can also deepen the experience, and by more fully involving both participants, elements of *team creativity* are introduced. Partners can have the adventure of creating a fantasy together.

The fantasy acceleration technique can be used in relation to many of the duo-games in this book. The method seems to work best if a three-minute egg timer is used. Flip a coin to see which partner first embarks on a particular fantasy adventure. As the winner begins the fantasy adventure, the other partner starts the egg timer. *The egg timer should be out of the line of vision of the player* as in many instances the person sharing a fantasy who is watching the "sands of time" run out feels this as a form of pressure. By using the egg timer the strain of looking at a watch is avoided along with such comments as "you made a mistake in your timing."

For Beginning Players

When three minutes are up raise a hand to get your partner's attention. As soon as he stops (and he should stop shortly after he sees your hand signal), add some positive action embellishments of your own which fit in with his fantasy at this point. *The objective is to*

> *enhance the partner's fantasy,*
> *help him with his fantasy stream and story line,*
> *add details, richness or elaborate a point or theme.*

The purpose is not to add a new theme or incident in order to change the course or character of the fantasy. Nor is it an objective at this point to challenge the partner, or by the introduction of new elements, stimulate the exercise of his ingenuity.

For the beginning player of fantasy games the fantasy acceleration technique should be used only to enhance and foster the partner's unfolding fantasy adventure.

Example:

> Del R. had begun playing the gypsy fantasy game (see page 36). He decided to take a boat to India rather than fly, described the interior of the luxury cruiser, mentioned a floating garden and described a brief storm which was weathered safely.

At this point the egg timer ran out, and Jane, his partner, began:

> "The beautiful floating garden in the boat was filled with ferns and orchids and there was a small waterfall. . . ." *(adding detail* or richness). Del then had the boat land in India, visited a raja and went into the jungle for a hunt."

At this point the egg timer again ran out and Jane said,

> "The jungle offered many opportunities for observing animals or hunting. Elephants were available and natives were ready to build platforms in the trees."

(Jane's *elaboration of a point or theme,* gives Del a springboard for his *fantasy to take it where he wanted.)*

For Advanced Players

After you have successfully played quite a number of fantasy games, the following can be used to accelerate the flow of the fantasy stream:

At the end of a three-minute period determined by the egg timer, Jane could point to or hold up one to three objects such as a tree, a flower, a glass (any object will do) which John will then incorporate into his fantasy. (Jane points to an oak tree and rose.)

Example: Del said,

> "The raja showed me an oak tree he had brought over from the campus of the school he attended. He then told me a story about a rose he had grown in his garden."

Details or new elements can be added by the partner which are in general agreement with the broad plot line and flow of the fantasy and which stimulate the use of creative ingenuity. These can be fantasy subthemes or fantasy stimulators.

Example: Jane said,

> "Suddenly there was a silence in the jungle; then came a soft sigh as the wind passed the tree tops, and suddenly, as if by magic, there was a huge tiger in the clearing right in front of you."

John now has to deal with this situation. It would have violated his plot line if Jane had unexpectedly called in a tornado to spoil his stay in the jungle before it even got started.

Again, the objective of fantasy subthemes or fantasy stimulators is to facilitate the partner's fantasy adventure and to participate and have fun at the same time. The objective is never to confound him, do violence to his fantasy or force him into a corner. For this latter purpose a special, the fantasy challenge (see page 38) can be used. This game is recommended for experienced fantasy players.